Extraordinary stories of survival, courage and heroism

JOYCE NG

HOTEL 9/11

AN ORAL HISTORY FROM SURVIVORS OF
3 WORLD TRADE CENTER

Foreword By
NATIONAL SEPTEMBER 11 MEMORIAL & MUSEUM

ISBN 978-0-9978605-1-1

JSW Books
PO Box 3311
Fayville MA 01745

**JSW
BOOKS**

September 2016
First Edition

For all the survivors who witnessed and escaped tragic events,
we move on despite bearing witness to the worst of humanity.
No one understands why one person survives while another does
not. But for those who do survive, there is a duty to honor,
remember, and serve as a witness for all those who didn't.

It is our duty as survivors to be the voice
for those who are no longer with us.

ABOUT THE HOTEL

The Marriott World Trade Center hotel was inside the World Trade Center complex and connected the North and South towers. On September 11, 2001, there were approximately 1000 registered guests.

The hotel was destroyed as a result of the collapse from the North and South Towers.

- The collapse of the South Tower destroyed the center of the hotel.

- The collapse of the North Tower destroyed the rest of the hotel.

There were people who died in the hotel, including firefighters, employees and hotel guests. Fourteen people who had been trying to evacuate the partially destroyed hotel after the first collapse managed to survive the second collapse.

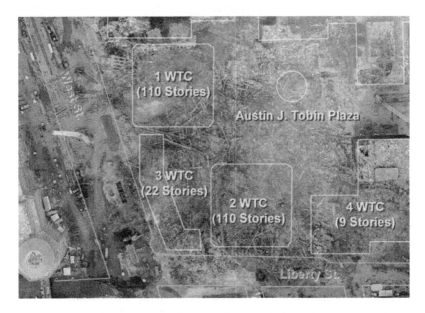

Aerial view after the September 11 attacks
(Federal Emergency Management Agency, Public Domain)

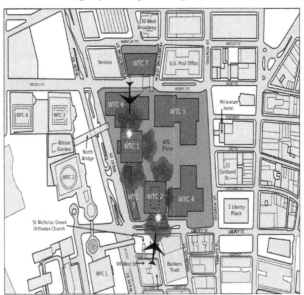

World Trade Center Layout and surrounding buildings
(Federal Emergency Management Agency, Public Domain)

For my husband
and daughter

CONTENTS

FOREWORD

By Joe Daniels
President & CEO
National September 11 Memorial & Museum

On the morning of September 11, 2001, the New York Marriott World Trade Center was operating normally. Hospitality staff went about their usual morning responsibilities, ensuring a pleasant stay for their 940 guests, and men and women on business trips prepared for meetings and conferences while vacationers planned their day of sight-seeing in New York City. No one yet knew that the events of this particular Tuesday morning would irreversibly alter their lives, let alone the entire world.

Often, when we think about large scale, historical events like 9/11, the lives and stories of individual people can get lost within the larger picture. It is easy to look at a headline and conjecture on the broad impact of a particular event or analyze a chapter in a history textbook fifteen years later simply through the lens of its impact on current global events without considering the human toll. These are actions that many of us take every day. Too many horrible disasters happen around the world, both natural and man-made, that it is unfathomable for us to attempt to internalize the effects on a single life or comprehend what it was like to live through such an ordeal.

These individual stories get rolled up together to create a simple, easily understood narrative, but it is imperative that this historical treatment not be applied to the attacks of September 11. Through hearing and reading personal stories from major world events like 9/11, we are reconnected with our shared humanity. Much of the time, history happens around us but every so often, history happens to us. In those cases, first-hand accounts personalize the event for others, reconnecting survivors with the world around them and creating much needed depth and context for those who listen.

On the morning of September 11, nearly 3,000 people were brutally murdered after they simply boarded planes, went to work, or began their day at a hotel. Tens of thousands of others, however, survived. In the haze and confusion of that morning, men and women banded together to make it down crowded stairwells often assisted by the direction of first responders. These men and women are who we are: mothers, fathers, sons, daughters, brothers, and sisters. This is why understanding their stories is so important. The stories of what happened in the hours during and after the attacks highlight the potential each of us has for goodness. Each of these are tremendous illustrations of how individual perspectives can improve not only our way of viewing the history of that day, but our way of viewing our fellow man.

Within these pages you will read some of these types of stories from the survivors of the World Trade Center Marriott Hotel. Directly from the people who lived through the attacks, you will read remarkable accounts of hotel guests persevering through unfamiliar surroundings in the midst of immense terror and confusion, hotel employees helping to evacuate guests, firefighters responding to guide civilians through the danger. The survivors who share their stories here, and the thousands of others who escaped that day, provide crucial insight into the events of 9/11. Through them, we know of the bravery of the first responders, the professionalism of employees, and the compassion shown by perfect strangers. Through them, we know the story of 9/11 is more than just the story of terror and destruction that gripped the world's attention. Through them, we know the actions taken in response to the attacks exhibit the best we have to offer one another, even in the very worst circumstances.

And that is a history worth preserving.

Joe Daniels
President & CEO
National September 11 Memorial & Museum

AUTHOR'S PREFACE

September 11, 2001 was a defining day in my life. I was only a few years out of college, traveling to New York City for my first consulting assignment in the Financial District. I always chose to stay at the Marriott World Trade Center (or Three World Trade Center), which was nestled in between the gleaming twin towers.

That Tuesday was a turning point in my life and changed everything for me, as it did for thousands of others who were there. Three World Trade Center was one of the seven buildings destroyed on 9/11.

I was inside my hotel room when the first plane crashed into the North Tower. The landing gear of the plane crashed into the roof of the hotel and the hotel caught on fire. The building was subsequently destroyed when the towers collapsed on top of it. Through my escape, I saw people getting killed and injured. It was a terrifying day. I never expected to survive.

A few days after the attack, I wrote my account and sent it out to my colleagues, family and friends. My story was widely circulated. Other survivors from the hotel contacted me and wanted to connect. We created an informal group of "hotel survivors." Many of us have bonded over our shared experience. It was healing to connect with other survivors who shared this uncommon bond. We needed to share our stories and put some meaning behind what we experienced.

This group of "hotel survivors" meets regularly. On the anniversary, we hold a commemoration in New York. We travel from all over the country to meet so we can share our experiences with each other. Over lunch, we talk, laugh, cry, and share our personal experiences. We honor the heroes and remember the sacrifices made. More importantly, we also celebrate surviving. We celebrate moving on despite seeing the worse in humanity. Although our bond is born out of tragedy, it is a bond that ties us for life.

As a survivor, I have given speeches to schools and organizations about my experience. I have strived to educate the public on the impact of terrorism and its aftermath. I have talked to our nation's leaders, and given a voice to survivors. That way, we can promote the improvement of lives for those living with lingering emotional and physical trauma.

More importantly, in the course of forming the survivors' organization, my life crossed paths with a wonderful group of individuals. Throughout the process of working on the book, I felt so interconnected to the lives of these individuals that I often found it difficult to detach myself from their narratives for the purpose of this book. The emotional scars of 9/11 are inconceivable

Many survivors exposed fresh wounds by reliving their experiences with me. Through hours of interviews, we have shared tears as we walked through some of the most horrific moments in our lives. I can still feel the magnitude of the loss years later. I knew we had to write a book to preserve what we witnessed. I have listened to many heart-wrenching stories, all of which have been consolidated into these pages.

This book is unique because it tells of the events that happened in an overlooked building.

I feel honored to be involved in something so profound. I also never expected my life to intersect with some of the most wonderful, bravest and nicest people I have ever met.

I want to thank all the survivors, firefighters, and family members who opened their hearts and souls about a day we will never forget. They have made this book, an oral history of America's worst tragedy, a reality. And now they share it with you.

Living Past September 11

The morning of September 11, I was inside my room (Room 1335) at the WTC Marriott when Flight 11 crashed into the North Tower. Debris from the first tower was falling in and around the area. As a result, the hotel caught on fire. I, and many others, had to flee the burning building. People were running in all directions, frightened, panicked, some getting injured. It was a terrifying day.

While I was outside, the second plane flew over my head. I watched it crash into the South Tower while I was standing inside the World Trade Center near the door. The images and sounds will be forever etched in my memory. It was one of the saddest days in my life.

Many years later, my memory of September 11 is acute but fragmented. Some of it is captured in my mind with remarkable clarity, some in sounds, smells or other sensations only a person who was there can understand. Other pieces have been deposited and locked in my head, refusing to resurface until they are triggered by another memory.

I kept my hotel key from the Marriott Hotel at 3 World Trade Center and store receipts from the World Trade Center shops. They are now displayed in the National 9/11 Memorial and Museum. I also have my mental image of the wonderful view from my hotel room looking out at the river, and seeing the plaza with the sculpture. I also have my mental image of the gleaming Twin Towers, and the incredible rush of humanity passing through the plaza each day. The Twin Towers looked so tall; they seemed to blend into the sky. I remember the bronze statue of the businessman named Double Check that steadfastly refused to move, even after the attack.

This memory bears no resemblance to what remained after the September 11 attacks. It is changed forever.

I find it difficult to convey the intensity of emotions and feelings I experienced that day without sounding like I am not "handling it." As a whole, those who escaped from the attacks are a neglected group. Not many people are sympathetic to the lifelong trauma that exists for survivors. However, we shouldn't be marginalized because we survived. The worry of being forgotten weighs heavily, however irrational this feeling is. I want people to remember. I need to remember for myself to put meaning behind what I experienced.

My journey as a survivor is a mixture of denial, an aspiration to live life completely, a desire to help others, and also a deep sadness of the lives lost that day. A few days after September 11, I wrote my account and sent it to my friends, family and colleagues. Afterwards, I never wrote about it again. I wanted to forget and move on. I was afraid to dredge up all those feelings and thoughts again. How do you explain what it is like witnessing mass murder and bloodshed?

But since then, I have read many collections of individual narratives from survivors and often fought back tears as I read those stories. Years later, I continue to speak with survivors and hear their stories. When I started creating my non-profit charity to help others, I realized I needed to start recording my thoughts and all the stories of those who survived.

I spent months replaying the death and destruction in my head. I spent months not being able to sleep peacefully. I wondered how I survived when others didn't. I will never forget what I saw. I thought about the vulnerability of life and was grateful I survived. I knew I was given a second chance.

I was able to return home, but many people were not. When I returned home, and people learned I was at the World Trade Center, inevitably their first question was *"Which tower were you in?"* They didn't know there were seven buildings in the World Trade Center. Most didn't know that the twin towers were connected by a hotel - the Marriott World Trade Center, or as it has since become known, Hotel 9/11.

For people who were not affected by September 11, there is a huge disparity between what I experienced that day compared to what is seen on television and media. This disparity is evident in people's comments.

People say, "You were smart to leave the building."

I respond with,

"Smart has nothing to do with me getting out. I was just lucky to have left at the right time in the right place, where no debris fell on me outside. In fact, at that moment, it may have been smarter to stay inside because there was risk of getting killed by falling debris outside."

People say, "You should forget about this and put it behind you."

I respond with,

"Yes, I escaped and am moving forward with my life. But how do you explain the feeling of having survived when so many others didn't. Being a survivor and bearing witness to death is not something you can forget easily. Being a 9/11 survivor will always be part of me."

When the 9/11 anniversary approaches and I walk around with a heavy heart, people ask, "Who did you lose?"

My response is "I lost part of myself on September 11."

Timeline of Events

September 11, 2001

On September 11, 2001, four coordinated attacks occurred in the United States. The attacks killed nearly 3000 people and injured thousands more. It was the single largest loss of life for firefighters and law enforcement officers in the history of the United States.

All seven buildings in the World Trade Center complex were destroyed, including the hotel at Three World Trade Center, located at the base of the North and South towers.

Timeline of key events

7:59 am: American Airlines Flight 11 departs from Boston to Los Angeles.

8:14 am: United Airlines Flight 175 departs from Boston to Los Angeles.

8:20 am: American Airlines Flight 77 departs from Washington DC to Los Angeles.

8:42 am: United Airlines Flight 93 departs from Newark to San Francisco.

8:46 am: American Airlines Flight 11 crashes into the North Tower (floors 93-99)

9:03 am: United Airlines Flight 175 crashes into the South Tower (floors 77-85)

9:37 am: American Airlines Flight 77 crashes into the Pentagon in Washington, DC.

9:59 am: The South Tower (2 WTC) collapses, 56 minutes after being struck

- The hotel (3 WTC) was crushed by the South Tower

10:03 am: Flight 93 crashes into a field in Pennsylvania

10:28 am: The North Tower (1 WTC) collapses, 102 minutes after being struck

- The hotel (3 WTC) was crushed by the North Tower

The remains of the Marriott World Trade Center hotel after the collapse.
The remains of the North Tower can be seen in the background of the hotel.
(Federal Emergency Management Agency, Public Domain)

Health Implications - Survivors from World Trade Center

The attacks on the World Trade Center left toxic debris that spread throughout Lower Manhattan. Exposure to toxins contributed to health issues for thousands of survivors and responders. Years later, thousands of individuals suffer from health implications from 9/11-related issues

September 11 Survivors of Three World Trade Center

September 11 Survivors of Three World Trade Center is a recognized nonprofit 501(c)(3) organization founded by survivors who escaped Three World Trade Center on September 11, 2001

Our organization includes all individuals affected by the events of September 11, including hotel survivors, hotel responders, hotel employees, hotel guests, family members, or anyone else who support our mission. Our mission is to increase the strength and resiliency of the survivors of Three World Trade Center and others who survived the attacks on September 11, 2001; to remember the sacrifices and the losses of that day; to promote the improvement of life for survivors; and to educate the public on the impact of terrorism and its aftermath.

We accomplish this by:

1. representing survivors' interests with the 9/11 memorials

2. promoting the improvement of life for survivors living with lingering emotional and physical impact

3. educating the public in schools and other communities on the impact of September 11, 2001

INTRODUCTION

THE MARRIOTT HOTEL was inside the World Trade Center with an address of Three World Trade Center. It is often forgotten in September 11 discussions. The hotel connected the North and South towers, and was destroyed when the towers collapsed. Nearly 1,000 guests were registered at the hotel that day. Many others were there to attend the conference or use the facilities. Approximately 50 people, mostly firefighters, died in the hotel.

The stories that took place in this building are still unknown, but they make up the extraordinary history of the day at the World Trade Center. This book is important because it focuses on a building that is overshadowed.

Since the hotel at Three World Trade Center was nestled between the twin towers, the lobby was the most obvious way to enter the World Trade Center and was where the firefighters arrived. Because of its pivotal location, the hotel lobby served as a staging area occupied by firefighters and police. It also served as the exit from the North Tower and a runway in and out of the burning towers. By using the hotel, survivors were able to leave the North Tower, without venturing outside on West Street and risk getting hit by plunging debris.

When the South Tower collapsed, the hotel was severed from top to bottom. In the hotel lobby, depending on where you were, firefighters, rescue workers, police, guests and employees were either caught in the debris, injured, killed or struggled to survive in the rubble.

The historical narratives in this book are compiled from this special group of survivors – a group of people that were in the same building, the Marriott Hotel on September 11. The book contains oral histories of escapes from first-person accounts. Together, these stories form a special and compelling history from the different lives that intersected that day.

These are individuals whose lives will be forever impacted by the horror and chaos they witnessed.

The memories of that day will never be extinguished. But as the years pass, memories fade and time can distort them. Before the memories fade, it's essential to preserve the voices of the people who were there.

The intent is to capture all the stories into a collection to preserve for history, and to hand down to future generations. To have history be told through first-person testimonials is essential and very powerful. *Hotel 9/11* helps preserve these powerful stories on this monumental tragedy in American history.

HOTEL SURVIVORS

Survivors' Gathering for 5 Year commemoration (2006)

Survivor Gathering 10-year commemoration (2011)

Survivor Gathering (September 2011) Joyce & Greg

Survivors 10 Year Gathering (September 2011) Matthew, Crystal & Joyce

Survivors Joyce Ng and Richard Stark (2014)

Acknowledgement

Thanks to all of the survivors, firefighters and family members who poured their hearts and souls to make this book a reality. I am indebted to every survivor who I have had the privilege to connect with. Over the course of forming the September 11 Survivors of Three World Trade Center charity, my life has intersected with some of the most amazing people I have ever met. They have become my extended family. Thanks to Bill and Laurel Vaughan, Frank Razzano, Richard Stark, Leigh and Faye Gilmore, Greg Frederick, Anulfo Ponce, Milcia Pena, FDNY Heinz Kothe, FDNY Jeff Johnson, FDNY Jason McGimpsey, Patrick Anderson, Father Engel, Matt Harttree, Denise Campbell, Crystal Cattano, Drew Porter and so many others I have connected with.

I would also like to thank my early board of directors who helped with the initial stages of the non-profit. Frank Razzano, I am grateful for your straight talk and legal guidance. Underneath the tough exterior, you have a heart of gold. To Bill Vaughan, whose gentle soul and moral support I will always value. You are a wonderful musician and I will always remember how your 9/11 inspired music touched everyone.

To Patrick Anderson, my counterpart in Michigan, who has dedicated much of his time to preserve the memories of 9/11 with his non-profit charity "*Michigan Remembers.*" You were one of the first survivors I talked to after 9/11. Thank you Patrick for your support and advice throughout the past years

To my friend, Leo Blume who believed in the mission of the 9/11 survivors.

To my friend Dave McLure, we became friends as a result of the Boston Marathon attacks. Although our bond was formed as a result of another tragedy, I am glad we became friends. Thanks for offering to help out any way you can in our mission.

To Sal Iannuzzi and Lise Poulos who also supported our mission to remember 9/11.

To David Hastings who helped me a great deal during the initial stages of forming a non-profit and always believed in the importance survivors play in history.

To Teresa Mathai from Mass 9/11 Fund, who is one of the strongest women in the 9/11 community and someone who I could always go to for advice.

Thanks to all the staff and volunteers from the 9/11 Tribute Center. I was one of the first volunteer docents when the Tribute Center was in its infancy. The community was valuable in that it enabled us to heal by allowing us to tell our stories. A shout out to Kim - you cared so much about the 9/11 community, including fetching a rescue puppy for a little girl. Thank you.

To Amy Weinstein, Jan Ramirez and Joe Daniels from the National September 11 Memorial and Museum - thanks for supporting the survivors' community and working with me over the years, including attending our gatherings.

I would like to thank my parents for their love and support.

To my husband, whose never-failing support, encouragement and love made this book happen. You have been a true partner every step along this difficult journey and we have done this together. None of the charity work, annual commemorations and creation of this book would have been possible without your unwavering love and support. You suffered tremendously on 9/11 when I went missing. But when we reunited, I saw the tears and look of hope in your eyes. You inspired me to write this book through your life-long thirst for knowledge and truth. Your compassion, dedication to public service, and unfaltering altruism will always serve as an inspiration in my life and the lives of others. And during those weekends I spent working on the book, thank you for being a supportive father.

To my daughter, I wrote this book for you. When you were six years old, you asked me an insightful question:

"How is war and killing other people supposed to bring peace in the world?"

Your thought-provoking question is the basis behind this book, and highlights an important perspective only the innocence of a child can provide. You may be too young to understand, but I started this project to ensure our stories are preserved for you and future generations. One day, you will grasp the importance of maintaining the history of 9/11 in order to make the world a more peaceful place.

It is our hope that the next generation can help promote peace and tolerance in the world.

When you saw me working on the book covers, you said, *"Mommy I want to help make you a good cover."* Your covers were the most thoughtful of the bunch; thank you for seeing the beauty in everything.

The buildings shone in the sky.

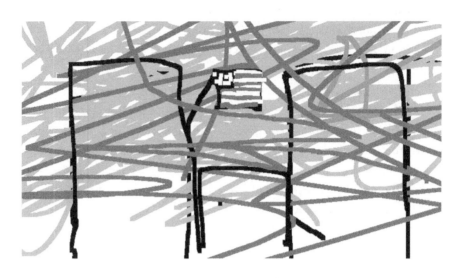

After September 11, the United States was shattered.

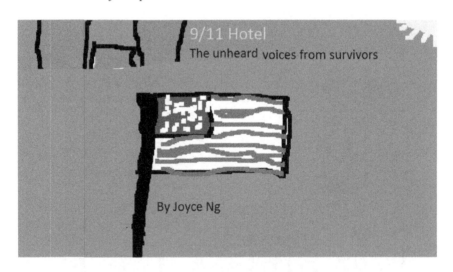

America will remain strong despite everything.

In memory of Todd Hill, James Cleere and Brett Owen Freiman,
the registered guests who died in the hotel.

PATRICK L. ANDERSON
Ten Minutes to Escape for a Michigan CEO

Patrick Anderson is the CEO of Anderson Economic Group. He is from Michigan and was staying on the 5th floor of the hotel inside the World Trade Center. On the morning of 9/11, he was attending an economics conference in the hotel when the attacks occurred. Patrick and a co-worker escaped before the hotel collapsed under the falling towers. Since then, Patrick founded Michigan Remembers, a 9/11 charity that preserves the memories of the 19 people from Michigan who lost their lives.

"PERIODICALLY, WE HEARD THE AWFUL SOUND OF SOMETHING THAT WAS NOT INANIMATE. IT WASN'T A BUILDING OR A PIECE OF A PLANE. IT WAS SOMETHING WITH A PURPOSE AND A LIFE. WE KNEW, BUT DID NOT WANT TO KNOW, THAT THE TERRIBLE SOUND MEANT THAT LIFE HAD ENDED."

Ten Minutes to Escape

I grew up in a small town in Michigan, and didn't want to live in the big city. However, by some manner of divine providence, I found myself at the World Trade Center on September 11, 2001, and survived to return home—unlike many others, including others who risked and lost their lives to give me a chance to escape.

For that reason, I have joined with survivors and patriotic Americans to remember that day, the heroism and the loss. In Michigan, the Michigan Remembers 9-11 Fund annually sponsors a Run to Remember, and every day remembers the Michigan victims of this tragedy. We share the mission of the Marriott World Trade Center Hotel Survivors to ensure that the history of this day, and the remembrance of the victims, continues onward.

This story is a remembrance of ten minutes at the World Trade Center that day, beginning about five minutes after the first plane hit. For some of the people mentioned, I know whether they lived or died; for others, I may never know. However, the story should be told.

The Crash of a Thousand China Cabinets

At 8:47, I was in my hotel room at the Marriott. I had been on the top of the building just 25 minutes earlier, but had come down after—ironically—complaining that I couldn't find a stairway down. As I learned later, parts of the plane that hit the first tower fell through the ceiling of the Marriott. Coming downstairs before then was the first brush with death for me that day.

When the plane did hit, I felt the building sway, in a manner that could not be explained. I heard a sound like the crash of a thousand china cabinets falling over. Looking outside, I could already see fire, debris, and death. Inside, I could feel doom. Still, it was another several minutes before I left the room—encouraged, perhaps, by the announcement to "stay in your rooms" that played over the loudspeaker. When I did leave, I had one shoe on, and one shoe off, and left everything I had brought to the city except my wallet, cellphone, and pocketknife. I didn't know it then, as I began running down the stairwells, but I needed every second I had.

The Useless White Suitcase

Down I went in the staircase, pausing only to put one shoe on and lace it quickly. As I got toward the second floor, more people joined me in the stairwell. Soon, I burst out of the interior staircase, now joined by dozens of others, swelling into hundreds of people escaping from both towers who had entered WTC 3. They were confused, scared, agitated—and remarkably uncertain about what had already happened. Many attempted to talk on cellphones, which were already failing to work. It didn't stop stories from spreading; the most emphatic, told to me by a man who appeared to know, was "a Cessna hit the tower." Having already heard, and felt, the impact of the first plane, I didn't believe that assertion—but I hoped it was close to true.

On the second floor, there was a large, semi-circular staircase that led to the first floor lobby. There was now a full-scale exodus in place, and dozens of people moved hurriedly toward the staircase and down it. Outside the window, we could see debris fall in an irregular rain, some wafting down in a black, circular death wallow.

As I went down the staircase, a woman walked irregularly next to me, struggling in her panic to carry a white suitcase. She was old, and she was hyperventilating so much I thought she might fall over at any moment. The suitcase was very important to her—so important she was struggling to carry it, even as precious moments ticked away.

I turned to her and spoke directly to her face, in a way you do when you are thrown together with others who are in the same peril.

"We're going to live. Let's just walk out of here." Then I took the suitcase from her hand, and carried it down the stairway. It was heavy.

At this time, I still didn't know how much of a peril we were in. I felt the doom, but still hoped the "Cessna hit the tower" assertion was true.

At the bottom of the stairway, I handed the burden back to her. We were now moving slowly, and she could briefly rest the suitcase if she needed to. Later that day I wondered what was so valuable in the suitcase, and why she would risk her life struggling to carry it out of a burning building. I later decided that, if I had known what lay ahead, I would have thrown the suitcase away and told the woman nothing in it could possibly be worth losing her life.

The crowd now swelled to two hundred or more. We were in the first floor lobby of the Marriott World Trade Center, or WTC 3. People leaving the tallest towers were arriving by the minute, as were others from trains elsewhere in the complex. It was about 8:55 am, and the first plane had hit the North Tower just 8 minutes ago. As we learned later, the South Tower occupants hadn't yet received a formal evacuation order

Three NYFD firemen were there. They announced sternly that we should proceed toward the south entrance, where they were sending groups running across Liberty Street. The front of the building—facing the West Highway—was too dangerous to enter, as debris continued to fall don, as well as large objects that, we could sense, was much more than debris.

We moved, steadily, toward the doors; periodically, another group would sprint across the street to the south of the WTC complex. It couldn't have been more than 6 minutes; it is frozen in time for me like it was 60.

The Fireman's Last Carry

As I waited, a woman fainted (perhaps she was the woman with the white suitcase; I'll probably never know.) The tallest of the three firemen picked her up over his shoulder in a fireman's carry, and shouted "gangway." I looked straight into his eyes, which were very brown, and very determined. The crowd parted for him, and he ran out with her over her shoulder.

I realized later, and it brings tears to my eyes as I wrote this, that after he carried that woman across the street, he came back into the building to help more people get out. There, he died, probably when the second of the two tallest towers collapsed onto the Marriott World Trade Center. The lobby of the WTC Marriott was buried so deeply under the rubble of three buildings that they didn't find his body until January 1 of the following year.

I think about this from time to time; a thousand of us walked in once and ran out once; this man ran in twice. He could not have misunderstood what he was doing; all of us felt the impending doom and knew that building was going to fall that day. Yet he did not abandon his post or neglect his mission. I never met his family, and I hope one of them one day reads this story and knows the heroism of his last hour. I dedicated a book I wrote a few years later to the memory of these three men.

The Final Volition

I waited my turn in the crowded lobby, more people poured in from the two tallest towers, from the Marriott, and as I learned later, even from the transit hub underneath the center. The scene outside the windows was surreal, as bits and pieces of the burning building above fell down. Sounds of banging, and yelling, and of sirens, and stressful voices, and footsteps and hard breathing filled the air. Periodically, we heard the awful sound of something that was not inanimate, that wasn't a building or a piece of a plane, that was something with a purpose and a life. We knew, but did not want to know, that the terrible sound meant that life had ended.

I cannot plumb the depths of despair and horror that must have moved them to take their final step, high above, facing death on all sides. I cling to a thread of hope, or perhaps a speculation about the serenity of a man's final decision, that at the very end they chose volition.

The Plane that Shouldn't Be Overhead

The crowd pressed forward toward the south-facing doors. More debris fell down. It was nearly my turn to run. I knew that once out of the doors, whatever came down from the sky could land upon you.

It was my turn. I sprinted south. Suddenly, I heard another sound, very loud; it was the screaming of a low-flying jet plane. I looked up, and saw the second plane coming right over my head. I thought immediately that the plane was in the wrong place; that it was too low; that the flight controllers couldn't possible send the plane there. And then I realized the true horror: that the hijackers were trying to fly the plane into the building; that the plane was going to fly into the building; and that everyone of the plane and many more people in the building were going to die. Probably for everyone in America that day, there was the moment you realized what was truly happening. As I realized the plane, now banking as it rifled toward the tower, was being piloted for this very purpose, one second stretched to many seconds as my mind recoiled from the knowledge. I was running, the plane was flying, people were screaming, but time crawled as the darkness of evil men flooded my senses.

At this point, I thought I would probably die, too. The plane would hit the tower just behind me; fuel and building and plane parts would spill across the area, and the building would fall down. I was sure of all these things, and sure that if I remained in the street, I would die, either immediately or soon. I shouted, to nobody in particular, two words: "Not Good."

The Turn in the Road

I then did something unusual. I changed direction, and instead of running South, I turned a sharp right, and ran across the West Highway. Somehow, I calculated that I had five seconds to get underneath something that would protect me from the debris of the impact of the second plane—one more second before the plane hit, and then four seconds for the debris to hit. I began counting down in my head as I ran across the West Highway: 5, 4, 3… At this point, I ran around a bunch of other people who had chosen the same escape path. My mind was completely focused on escape, so much that I cannot recall hearing any sounds or feeling any sensation. There was a pedestrian bridge there, and I was nearly under it. My now fully functioning brain told me that that bridge was not going to stop a building from falling on me, so I kept running.

The Prayer Under the Truck

I reached the other side of the highway, and lo and behold, a large truck was parked there next to the World Financial Center. I can only remember one detail; it was a Mack truck that had a round headlight in a large rectangular frame, probably a garbage truck. I ducked under it. There were two other men also under the truck; their eyes were wild with fear. They said nothing. In my mind, I played out what was happening: the plane's impact, the debris falling, and the building staggering. I wondered whether the building would fall now, or soon. If it falls now, I told myself, I am dead now. If it falls later, I can still escape.

I prayed for that escape. I began saying the Lord's Prayer out loud, in front of the two terrified men. "Our Father, who art in heaven…" I started. When I finished the prayer, I said "Lord, please save me, and these other two guys with me!"

The men said nothing. When you are in the middle of death, nobody objects to a prayer.

I had now spent a minute under the truck. I told myself that, as I wasn't yet dead, the building hadn't fallen yet. I looked to my left, and the drive shaft was spinning several inches away. I realized the two men had probably been working, saw the plane hit the tower, and jumped under the truck while the engine was still running. I'm glad they didn't drive away; they gave me a shelter for the several seconds during which, I learned later, debris and jet fuel sprayed on the streets.

I also hope my prayer was heard for all three of us under that truck. It was heard for me; I was able, days later, to rejoin my family in Michigan. However, my wife endured four hours of not knowing whether I was alive or dead, and seeing plenty of evidence on TV that it was probably the latter.

It was also four hours later that I found my coworker, unharmed. He was on the second floor and left immediately, along with most of the other economists that had gathered for the NABE conference that day. He is now a US citizen, joining the country that had been attacked that day and where so many had died.

For many others, however, their anguished prayers were not rewarded in this life, and their loved ones did not return. This sadness will be with me for the rest of my life. So, too, will be the gratitude for the heroism of those that helped me and so many others escape.

JAMES CALECA

A man from Michigan deals with survivor's guilt

James Caleca was traveling from Michigan on a business trip. He was a guest in the hotel staying on the 8th floor. He describes the day as horrifying, frightening and disturbing. To this day, he is stricken with disbelief that he was lucky enough to survive the attacks while so many others died.

"THE EVENTS OF THAT DAY LEFT A SCAR ON OUR COLLECTIVE PSYCHES THAT WILL NEVER FULLY HEAL."

AFTER EXITING THROUGH the Marriott lounge doors onto Liberty Street, I went across from the World Trade Center at an angle that allowed me a view of both towers. I was absolutely stunned and horrified by the sight of the North Tower on fire and instinctively began thinking that I had to get out of Manhattan before things got worse.

My first inclination was that a bomb had exploded, and as I tried to call my wife and my office, I overheard a passerby say that a plane had hit the building. This gave me a tiny bit of relief thinking that maybe it was, in fact, an accident. This minor relief was immediately replaced with instant horror at the sight of bodies falling from the WTC.

As I stood in shock at the unbelievable sight before me, I witnessed the attack on the second tower. My horror turned into an indescribable terror at the instant realization that this was a deliberate act. From my perspective at street level, the second plane looked like a cruise missile and I thought that the United States was under attack. It was traveling so fast and slammed into the building with such force that I did not see the wings of the jetliner. I immediately turned and ran towards Battery Park. While repeatedly trying to reach my wife and my office, I tried to think of how I could get out of Manhattan. I knew that if I could reach New Jersey, I could rent a car and drive home. My only focus was getting to my family, but I didn't yet know that it was two planes that had caused this carnage.

When I reached Battery Park, I heard someone say that it was a plane that had hit the second tower, and I challenged them that it was a missile. They said that they had seen the plane themselves. I felt sick to my stomach thinking that this was a terrorist act, and within minutes heard on a radio that the Pentagon had been hit as well. My despair and fear grew. I didn't know anyone in New York and kept thinking that the situation was only going to get worse. I asked someone how to get out of the city and was told that all bridges and subways were closed and that the ferry boats were not running. I did learn, however, that the ferry boats departed from right near where I was, so I made my way towards that area.

Within 10 to15 minutes, a ferry boat arrived and I was fortunate enough to make it on. As I was boarding, I heard a loud rumbling noise and realized that it was getting very smoky. As the boat began to pull away from the dock, it was completely engulfed in smoke and dust from, what I later realized, was the collapse of the first tower. While it was very difficult to breathe on the boat, it was nothing compared to what those endured who did not make it on that first ferry boat. Nor was it as uncomfortable as it must have been for anyone in closer proximity to the disaster.

After I reached Staten Island, I was able to make some phone calls. Through my business association with my company, I made it to the local distributor who assisted me in finding a hotel in East Brunswick, NJ. They were gracious enough to give me a ride there at approximately 3:30 PM.

After I checked in, I turned on the TV and watched, along with the rest of the world, the news account of this tragedy. I could not believe that I had witnessed it.

I was emotionally drained and frightened. I had feelings of disbelief at having been there, and knowing the incredible good fortune of getting out when I did.

I was able to find a car to rent the next afternoon.

At approximately 1 PM on Wednesday, September 12th , I began the drive back to my home in the suburbs of Detroit, Michigan. I drove for 12 straight hours, only stopping for gas, and reached my home at 1 AM. I still couldn't believe I was there on that tragic day.

The past week has been a very difficult and emotional time. I am so incredibly grateful for having been able to escape the city when I did, yet I have also experienced strong feelings of cowardice for running away from it all. I don't know why I was spared the agony of dealing with the collapse of the towers. My heart aches for all the victims and their families. It not hard to fathom that this is only the beginning of a horror that may continue to unfold for quite some time.

The events of that day left a scar on our collective psyches that will never fully heal.

Aside from the time spent trying to reach my family and office through-out the ordeal, I was in constant prayer to God for guidance and strength. I do believe that I was blessed in that time of terror, and I fully realize that my emotional and psychological suffering was and is nothing compared to that of so many others. I pray for them all.

DENISE CAMPBELL
My Dear Man in the Tie

Denise Campbell was traveling from California to New York to meet prospective students when the attacks occurred. She was staying in the hotel at the World Trade Center in Room 2018. Her story is dedicated to the Man in the Tie whom she saw jump to his death. After 9/11, Denise suffered from enormous survivor's guilt. She developed a fear of heights and became apprehensive of flying, which she had to conquer in order live her life fully. It took her 28 days to get back home from New York.

"YOU WERE FALLING, FLYING REALLY, FROM THE SOUTH TOWER I BELIEVE. YOU FELL ALONE IN A DARK SUIT AND LIGHT-COLORED TIE. YOU HAD DARK HAIR AND LIGHTER SKIN. AFTER YOU, THERE WERE MANY MORE - TOO MANY. SOME ALONE, SOME TOGETHER, BUT TOO MANY. I ACHED."

MY NAME IS Denise Campbell. I was working for the University of Southern California in 2001 and traveled to New York to meet prospective students on the 11th of September. It took me 28 days to get home after the terrorist attacks, and I met many angels who helped me find hope and navigate my emotions during each stop along the way.

My life has changed dramatically over the years. In 2001 I was angry. I was hurt and possessed extreme survivor's guilt post 9-11. I was mad that these beautiful, unassuming people had to die. I was angry at the loss of our men and women in uniform – firefighters, police officers, men and women in the military. I could not comprehend why a group would attack our country. I was a control freak. I was jittery. My adrenals were shot, but I could run a marathon. I couldn't relax and I was afraid of heights.

Between 2002 and 2003, my anger resided. I felt a sense of duty to share the stories of those who lost their lives that day. I did not know them, yet I saw many of them perish, and they are the most profound part of my story. I want to be certain they are not forgotten.

I lived in Los Angeles at the time and was able to connect with a variety of groups and speak about survivorship and its responsibilities from my lens. I became less of a control freak and wasn't quite as jittery. I had no idea my adrenals were shot and that I wasn't as overly energetic as the year prior.

I still didn't like heights, but I visited tall buildings, stayed in high level hotels and even boarded the USS Topeka Submarine for a six hour tour and practice dive. I was learning to face my fears and reach for courage when I needed to. I flew on planes when necessary.

Over time, I realized the story and experience had nothing to do with me: I simply became the vehicle to share what happened. The point of my surviving was to help share the message of remembrance and hope with others, to remind us all that we are living with the gift of precious time.

Today, I live each day with gratitude and wonder, in hopes that those individuals will not have died in vain. I am not perfect. I am flawed. I make mistakes and mess up. I don't do everything perfectly, and there are days I fail to reach my objective of carrying gratitude and seeing the wonder of this thing called life. But somehow I pick myself up and readjust, putting those who have died in the forefront of my mind. I'm always reminding myself to live with love and to give love with grace the best way I know how to. I will always remember.

My dear Man in the Tie,

I am writing this to you and can't even address the letter correctly. I do not know your name. I do not know exactly what you looked like. I don't know if you have children or if you were married. But even without your name or a moment of spoken word, you are more meaningful to me than I can describe. At least you've changed and healed me forever.

You were working. I was sleeping. I woke up to a startling noise. A crash. The floor moved. The first plane hit. A huge wave threw me out of bed. I thought it was an earthquake. You were probably shocked. Maybe you were on the phone, checking your email or writing a proposal. Maybe they told you to stay in the building or you didn't think you needed to get out. You were on a higher floor. You wouldn't get out in time.

I was in the Marriott World Trade Center (3 WTC). I had arrived from Los Angeles the night before. I ran downstairs and outside, in my bright red pajamas. I couldn't breathe I was running so fast. Maybe you had heard an announcement that it was okay for you to stay in your office. Or maybe you didn't want to leave. Others evacuated anyway, but maybe you were not frightened. Or maybe you couldn't get out. Maybe you were courageous.

I ran across the street as a second plane flew into the South Tower. It disappeared completely. I froze. You probably did too. Maybe you felt the ground underneath you shake. Maybe for the same moment in time our breath stopped. That was your building that was hit. The second one. I stared in amazement. I held hands with a stranger in a light blue suit. She squeezed my hand. A man next to me lost his arm due to a piece of flying debris.

You probably tried to run. I'm sure that it was hot. You were stuck on the side facing Liberty Street – I think. There was nowhere for you to go. You seemed to come from the origin of the fire. I suppose it was too hot for you. There was a lull outside. People were speculating, trying to figure out what was happening. Quick words, no sentences. There was debris falling, smoke pluming from the towers…and then, you made your decision. The fire was reaching for you, and then I saw you for the first time.

You were falling, flying really, from the South Tower I believe. You fell alone in a dark suit and light-colored tie. You had dark hair and lighter skin. The crowd was silent except for a unanimous sigh. That was all we could mutter as you fell. It seemed like hours that we watched you. After you there were many more. Too many. Some alone and some together. But too many. I ached.

I do believe your body fell to earth, but I'm sure that before the end of your flight, your soul soared above to meet so many others that were already there – and those who would join you in the following moments.

I dreamt of you for months. I could not see your face. Sometimes you were in the suit, sometimes I couldn't tell, but your tie was always upwards. You were beautiful even though I cannot describe you in full. In my dreams you came to me and I could always feel your presence. I wonder if that is you, in my dream, coming to greet me, introducing yourself. I wonder if you know that the pain of seeing you fly introduced a new thread of reality for me - a thread of anger, pain, guilt for living, worry, acceptance, devout respect, hope, love, and of peace, finally peace.

I cannot wait to meet you. Though my time is not yet, I am no longer scared of the day when it will reach me – and that is because of you. I know many who are in heaven - family and friends from different parts of life. And I look forward to the day where I can meet their souls again. But mostly I can't wait to see you, meet you and look at your beautiful face. I paint your figure on soft white paper but leave the face blank, a canvas incomplete. You will be my first stop in eternity, where I can finally take your hand and greet you soul to soul. I will say thank you for changing my life and my perspective. I will say I have never forgotten you and that you were my daily reminder to live with love. My unlikely hero, I love you so.

Denise (2002)

CRYSTAL PEDONE-CATTANO
My toe rings may have saved me

Crystal Pedone-Cattano was a consultant traveling to New York City on business. She was staying in Room 2121 at the WTC Marriot hotel. In the past year, she had become a regular guest at the Marriott, staying there on a weekly basis for nearly a year. On September 11, she left her hotel room later than usual due to interesting circumstances. She was able to evade death and believes her toe rings played a pivotal role in her good fortune.

"I BELIEVE IF I HAD GOTTEN ON THAT ELEVATOR 30 SECONDS TO ONE MINUTE EARLIER, IT COULD HAVE BEEN THE DIFFERENCE BETWEEN LIFE AND DEATH FOR ME."

Room 2121

9/11 Timeline

(5:30 am) Room 2121 - Marriott World Trade Center

My alarm clock went off at approximately 5:30 am, but I didn't actually roll out of bed until 5:45 am. I dressed into my workout clothes, piddled around with my music player for about 10 minutes too long and then headed towards the elevator that would take me up one floor to the hotel gym.

(6:05 am) 22nd Floor – Fitness American Gym

I arrived at the gym at approximately 6:05 am, signed in and headed towards the treadmill in the hypoxic training chamber for a quick run. I started my 2.5 mile run that overlooked a portion of Battery Park and an awesome marina that housed huge, beautiful boats and yachts. I remember how stunning the reflection of the sunrise was across the water this particular morning.

I used to tell myself that I could just keep running until I ran across the Hudson; I believed I could run on the building shadows from the morning sunrise, never stopping until I reached Jersey City. I loved thinking the morning sun had rolled out her magic water carpet just for me so I could finish my run.

I remember so vividly how "crisp" the morning appeared; how totally blue the skies were - not overcast or cloudy. I even remember thinking as I was cooling down, "Wow - what a beautiful day; fall weather is just around the corner."

(6:30 am) Room 2121 - Marriott World Trade Center

Before I get into too much detail, let me share a little bit of history. I had been a weekly resident of the Marriott World Trade Center since November 2000, arriving each Sunday and departing each Thursday week after week for almost a year. I was a software consultant working on Wall Street. I did not realize at the time how totally "routine" some parts of my life had been over the past 11 months. Upon check-in, I was usually given a Marriott junior suite (or better) each week. The Marriott staff, who had become family, always took care of me. The junior suites were located at the end of the hotel hallway (next to the stairwell exit) on the right side of the hotel. The rooms were huge and were primarily all windows. Most of the time, but not always, I stayed somewhere between the 16th and 19th floors and had never had any problems with the room doors or keys until this week. Here is where things get even more "different" for me on this day.

My room this week was number 2121 - right smack in the middle of the hotel. I had requested a duplex room the week before instead of the junior suite. Upon checking in on Sunday night, I was informed there were no "special" rooms available, not even one of my normal junior suites. I was told that I had been originally booked in one of the end junior suites but had to be moved to number 2121 last minute due to an attorney having to stay longer. Due to an unexpected extended litigation, files were left littered all over the room – which to me did not make sense to make anyone move rooms. Still, I agreed to the request and shrugged it off, thinking to myself, "It's no big deal; I needed a change anyway."

I finished my run at approximately 6:30 am and decided to return to my room and drop off my music player before going for my "routine" coffee run in the Concierge Lounge (my room this week was almost directly across from the stairwell exit that led down to the Concierge Lounge on the 20th floor.)

Looking back now, this is where my destiny would forever be changed.

(6:35 am) Room 2121 - Marriott World Trade Center

My room key would not work in my door. I thought this was weird, so I patiently returned to the elevators and went down to the main lobby. I was issued a new key.

(6:40 am) Concierge Lounge – 20th Floor - Marriott World Trade Center

On the way back up to the room, I decided to stop off on the 20th floor and pick up my morning coffee, just as I did every morning. I figured I had already wasted about 15 minutes with the key issue and needed to get moving since I had some emails to follow up on before leaving the hotel.

I entered the lounge around 6:40 am and found it to be very busy. I was usually the first hotel guest to arrive when the lounge opened at 6:30 am. Charles knew my schedule and would sometimes have my coffee waiting for me. This morning, I arrived almost 10 minutes later than normal.

The gentleman that had been on the gym treadmill before me was there and asked me how long I had been staying at the hotel. After a five-minute conversation about workout schedules, we exchanged a handshake and agreed he would arrive at the gym at 5:30 am and run for half an hour – so we could both get that cardio run into our morning workout. He mentioned he was staying at the hotel for 24 days and this was only his second day in NYC.

I still wonder how this stranger and my buddy Charles came out of all of this....

(6:50 am) Room 2121 - Marriott World Trade Center

My stupid room key STILL would not work in the door.

Instead of going back to the elevators and down to the main lobby again, I decided to use the hotel courtesy phone on my floor to call the front desk. I explained the situation and asked someone with a master key to please come up and let me into my room. The front desk said they would send someone right up.

(7:00 am) Room 2121 - Marriott World Trade Center

After 10 minutes, I walked back to the phone to call again. Just as I was dialing, the hotel security guy exited the elevator. I hung up the phone and as we were walking towards the room, he asked me my first and last name for verification and said he would need to see some sort of ID once I got into the room.

Well – long story short, his master key would not work either.

(7:05 am) Room 2121 - Marriott World Trade Center

I wish I could remember his name. He was so nice and apologized over and over again for the inconvenience as he communicated with his manager via walkie-talkie that an "E Key" (emergency key) was needed instead of the master key.

I remember telling him I had an early morning meeting and needed someone to hurry up with the "E Key" (he explained that the "E Key" overrode the privacy lock on the doors). He also mentioned he was leaving once I got squared away since his shift ended at 7:00 am.

(7:15 am) Room 2121 - Marriott World Trade Center

Another hotel staff member arrived with the "E Key" and was successful in opening my hotel room door. I never did have to show any ID…Funny the things we remember.

(7:20 am – 8:10 am) Room 2121 - Marriott World Trade Center

I changed out of my damp workout clothes and logged onto my email. At exactly 7:49 am, I emailed my weekly status report to all appropriate parties. At 8:07 am, I emailed a follow-up response to confirm dinner plans for the following week.

I then logged off and packed up that specific computer for the last time.

(8:10 am – 8:30 am) Room 2121 - Marriott World Trade Center

I jumped in the shower and started getting ready for work. I knew I was running at least 15 minutes behind schedule.

(8:30 am – 8:42 am) Room 2121 - Marriott World Trade Center

I changed clothes twice. I could not decide what I wanted to wear (as usual) and then messed with my "toe rings" for what seemed like a half an hour. I had been wearing the same toe rings on the same toes for months, and of all mornings when I was already running late, they had to start pinching me. What next?

I left my room for the elevator at approximately 8:42 am.

(8:42 am – 8:45 am) Marriott World Trade Center

On the way down from the 21st floor, I remember looking at my toes and thinking, "I can't believe how much time I spent messing with these stupid toe rings. Now I will have to wait to pick up another cup of coffee after my 9:15 meeting."

I had already pushed the button to get off the elevator in the main lobby, but decided I wanted to walk through the WTC Plaza on the 3rd floor since I was running late. Besides, it was so pretty outside. So, I pressed the PL (Plaza Level) button and was actually looking forward to the walk outside. The WTC plaza area was always setup for some lunch time show. I figured I would be back later for lunch. That did not happen.

Most mornings I usually go through the WTC Concourse to look at all the store windows on the way to work, but I knew (from previous experience) I could cut some time off my walk this morning by utilizing the WTC Plaza exit.

Knowing now what I didn't know then, I believe if I had gotten on that elevator 30 seconds to one minute earlier, it could have (and most likely would have been) the difference between life and death for me.

(8:45 am) Marriott World Trade Center

As I turned the corner of the elevator to enter the Plaza Level of the Marriott, I immediately knew something was wrong. I was standing in the center of that lobby, next to the glass banister, when dozens of people started rushing from the glass doors that exited to the WTC Plaza, the Greenhouse Cafe and the surrounding offices on that floor. I immediately FROZE – not in panic, but I think to gain some kind of understanding as to what was happening all around me. I can't explain it. I just knew that I was NOT going to follow any one of these people anywhere until I knew what was going on. Some people were racing down the spiral staircase, while some were racing past me towards the elevators I had just gotten off of. I couldn't be sure of anything at that point, except I wasn't going to jump off any "Brooklyn Bridge" just because everyone else was. I felt like I was in a slow motion movie, but I was the only person in moving in slow motion.

I remember these strange sounds coming from the WTC Plaza area, like light bulbs bursting at the rate of firecrackers…dull yet sharp and quick sounds. At first I thought the stage in the WTC Plaza (as I just mentioned, concerts were held there almost daily), had caught on fire and all the lighting equipment was exploding. It wasn't until I saw a man with blonde hair wearing a pink shirt come running through the glass door area, with what looked like his shirt and/or hair smoldering, that I knew something was SO NOT right.

Little did we all know that a hijacked Boeing 767 (American Airlines Flight 11) had just crashed into the north side of the North Tower of the World Trade Center at approximately the 93rd floor.

(8:47 am – 9:01 am) Marriott World Trade Center

As I started to move towards the spiral staircase that led down to the Marriott main lobby, I looked to my right and could not believe what I was seeing. The weird sounds outside now made perfect sense to me. It was almost like the actual thought process of; "Ah – now I get it" was going through my brain in that millisecond. I was hearing (and now seeing) huge burning chunks of gray/white cement slamming to the ground like rain up against the doors and restaurant windows – clouds of white dust and smoke were everywhere. I remember experiencing an overwhelming feeling of being "so totally alone" as I turned quickly to go down the stairs to the main lobby.

On the way down the stairs, a lady was shouting that it was a bomb. I am not a rude person by nature, but I did tell her to "please shut-up." I don't know how I knew this, but I just knew it WASN'T a bomb. She was starting to freak-out some of the other people who were trying to get down the stairs.

Once I could see out of the front hotel windows, I turned to her and another man behind me and told them to look at the debris. I could see a lot of twisted metal and concrete chunks falling with burning, charred papers – almost like confetti but ugly and dirty. I said the debris looked like it had come from an airplane and even mentioned that maybe there had been an airplane that had clipped one of the buildings.

Once down to the lobby level of the hotel, I remember seeing some people running from (and towards) the hotel entrance covering their heads from the falling debris. I made my way through all the dozens of people now entering the lobby, all the way to the lounge area where all the couches were located. I found an open area near one of the large main windows and stopped. I stood in front of a huge window and viewed the falling debris. I remember seeing two cops in front of the other tower entrance, standing outside their car, hands on hips, looking straight up, almost paralyzed. I started getting a little panicked at this sight because I knew the plane was close to one of the towers – and me.

My hands were shaking so badly that I could not dial my cell phone. I tried calling my office, then my husband, then my colleague/friend, Bill, who was also staying at the hotel. There were NO SIGNALS available.

I was near tears when I turned around, and who did I see? It was my colleague/friend, naked as a newborn except for his gym shorts and the shaving cream in his ears! He had no shirt, no shoes and no phone service. I can't begin to explain the relief I felt at that very moment. I remember asking Bill where Bernie was, and he said Bernie was on his way down from his room, right behind him. We were both looking out the windows - wondering what the hell had just happened - when out of nowhere, in an extremely crowed lobby, appeared Bernie, Tina and then Ragu. All the colleagues on my project! Wow! I remember later mentioning to Bill that we have more difficulties getting everyone together for a scheduled business meeting on most days than we did finding each other that morning.

I still believe, in all the excitement, that it was a "total miracle" that we found each other so quickly.

We all stood around for what seemed like a half an hour, talking about what we had seen or heard. Bernie had time to take off his business shirt and gave Bill the tank top he had on underneath. We even made jokes about this situation "so not working for me" and laughed at Bill for showing up in just his gym shorts with no shoes.

I did not feel we were in any danger and was definitely NOT in any hurry to leave because of all the debris still falling. I felt safer inside at this point.

No one had any idea that another hijacked Boeing 767 (United Airlines Flight 175) was less than two minutes away from crashing into the south side of the South Tower of the World Trade Center over our heads.

(9:01 am – 9:02 am) Marriott World Trade Center

I replay the next few moments over and over in my head often and still find I have missing pieces and time gaps.

Somehow, we started moving towards the Marriott Tall Ships Bar/Lounge with others in the lobby so we could be evacuated out the side entrance/exit door, the furthest exit from the other tower (the fire department had started asking everyone to evacuate quickly). I remember seeing and smelling a lot of dust in the lobby but did not smell any smoke until we started towards that exit route. Once we entered that area, I could see a lot of smoke coming from the kitchen. A Marriott staff member was standing near the stairs leading down and out of the bar, telling everyone to "exit quickly and to cover your head." Outside the exit was a police officer yelling at everyone to "run quickly and cover your heads." I asked the policeman on the way out what had happened, and he said it looked like a plane had crashed into the other tower. He again told me to cover my head and move quickly.

Once outside, I remember looking to my left. One of the first thoughts that ran through my brain was, "This would have been the other route I would have taken to work and it would have been so bad!!"

Huge pieces of concrete had smashed the rooftops of some of the cars and SUVs. Everything looked like it was covered in snow from all the dust and debris that had already fallen. I also recall thinking that EVERYTHING DID look like a bomb had gone off. I didn't want to see anymore and realized I had not covered my head because I had my rolling laptop case in one hand and my purse in the other.

We all ran across West Street to the opposite corner of the Marriott, near the South Tower. We stopped long enough to get everyone together, and Bill suggested we move further away since so much stuff was still falling from the sky. Some people were just standing around casually looking up at the North Tower burning. Hundreds of people were standing in the street after being evacuated from various buildings. I could see the top portion of the North Tower billowing with black smoke. Papers were falling and blowing around like snow.

I remember seeing what I thought was a person falling out of the top of the building, but immediately dismissed the thought. I told myself "There is no freaking way I saw what I just thought I saw," when two women behind me started crying hysterically. They said they had just seen someone fall from the top of the tower. I realized then what the loud, sickening thud noises were. I decided not to look up again. I still remember hearing all the cries from the bystanders each time someone else fell from the burning building.

I remember looking at two crying women as I turned to walk away with my colleagues. I thought, "What a terrible accident; there is just no way in hell this day could get any worse."

(9:02 am – 9:03 am) Marriott World Trade Center – West Street

I don't remember passing more than one road entrance after we moved from the first block across from the Marriott. However, I remember Tina pointing out how large some of the pieces of twisted metal were that had landed in the street as we walked away from the burning tower. I was wearing high-heeled sandals and still pulling my roller laptop case behind me – remember, I was on my way to work when this all started. I was trying to be conscience of where I was walking since there was so much debris to dodge (like a war zone), and I even remember calling out to Bill a few times to please be careful since he did not have any shoes on. I recall the pungent smell of burning paper, plastic and dust all around – a smell that will forever stay with me.

We stopped at the next block. We were approximately 100 to 150 yards from the South Tower now and this is where things are as unclear as they are clear and absolutely surreal. I cannot recall what we were talking about or if we were even talking at all—I think we were still just staring at the North Tower burning. Then, suddenly out of nowhere appeared an extremely LOUD, huge, ominous cloud that was flying low to the ground. I honestly thought (in that ½ a breath) that I could have jumped up high enough to touch the streaked metal belly. Deafening shrieks of whining metal broke out as the engines were rolled back and what seemed like the brakes were applied. The plane took a slight turn and then it was gone. It sliced through and disappeared into the South Tower.

Although my senses were in high gear, time appeared to stand still, yet it rushed through me like a nuclear blast. It was as if I was living a painfully slow, surreal horror movie, where my role was to stay calm in order to survive. The desire for self-preservation became the ultimate goal.

The shock of witnessing thousands of people dying in that second would not become real for me until a few days later.

I turned, dropped my laptop case and joined a human stampede that had already began to run towards Battery Park. I looked back only once when I felt I was far enough away from any falling debris. I remember seeing black smoke and orange fire billowing from the teal blue windows in such anger. I made a promise to myself not to look back again and hurried forward to catch up with the rest of my colleagues.

(9:04 am – 9:20 am) Battery Park

After catching up with Bill and Bernie and almost totally freaking out because they ran off and left me behind, we tried to find a "safe spot" to regroup. We found an area in Battery Park under some trees to stop and try to digest what was happening around us. My cell phone, just like everyone else's, would not pick up a signal. I sat down on a bench and remember all the different questions that were running through my head like a Wall Street stock banner:

What had just happened?
Was Manhattan under attack?
Who did this and why?
Should we stay away from the other buildings?
Would it be smart for us to be out in the open with large crowds?
Where would we be least vulnerable?

Bill suggested we get the hell out of Manhattan. We headed towards the Staten Island ferry to find Tina and Ragu. When we got there, we were told none of the ferry services were running. Bill then suggested we head towards the Brooklyn Bridge, which we could walk over the bridge and then find a place to meet his father to pick us up.

(9:20 am – 9:45 AM) Streets of New York City

I remember some really weird stuff. We were all pretty calm as we walked towards the South Street Seaport area. I noticed all the long lines for the pay phones and had no desire to stop and wait, all the papers on the streets, some had PeopleSoft panel shots and queries or were magazines that looked like they were from airplanes or business office waiting rooms with chard and burned edges. All the people standing around outside of the businesses and stores in the streets were like zombies. The smells of smoke and dust, as well as the sounds of ambulances and police cars and motorcycles, were everywhere. Paramedics and firefighters were coming from all directions. There was an overriding sense of confusion as to what had just happened. We agreed to stay together and respect everyone's mental and physical abilities until we could get out of Manhattan safely. "Leave no man behind" was our mentality.

Tina, Ragu and I had cell phones. We were continuously trying to get a signal so we could let everyone know we were ALL alright and find out about others. We decided to stop at a Duane Reade store on the corner of Broad Street at approximately 9:40 am to get water (I still have the receipt for my water!). I needed something in my stomach because I was starting to feel physically ill. This is when the reality of what I had just seen started to set in.

(9:45 am) Streets of New York City

Once outside again, we continued walking towards the South Street seaport area. Around 9:45 am, Tina's cell phone rang. We had her stop and stand still. Each one of us gave her boyfriend (Charlie) a number and a name to call to let that person know we were alright.

(9:45 am – 10:15 am) South Street Seaport

We all sat down near the Seaport ferries. I remember this young woman wanting to know if we were heading towards the Brooklyn Bridge. We all introduced ourselves and told her we were heading that way, and that she should stick with us. Bill and I discussed the safety of heading towards the bridge. I was concerned the bridges would be targeted next if the terrorists were trying to cripple the city. The lines for the seaport ferries were long, and no one appeared to be going in or out of the city via the ferries.

After a few minutes, we all stood up and headed toward the Brooklyn

Bridge. We hadn't gotten far at all when I heard loud crashing noises coming from the streets in front of us. People were running in all different directions trying to get away from the area. There is only one way to describe that scene in my mind: pure panic/mayhem. I was 100 times more terrified than I had been at any time that day. I thought bombs were going off on every side street in that area. The unknown ahead seemed more frightening than where we had come from. People were pushing and crowding where we were standing.

Tina and I took our shoes off, grabbed each other's hands and moved with the crowd towards the direction of the ferries. I could see Bernie and Ragu behind me, but I could not see Bill anywhere. A huge cloud of white dust limited our visibility to less than one block. By the time we all made it to the ferries, we were covered in white soot. We were trying to find Kleenexes to cover our mouths and noses. We were looking in all the ferry lines for Bill and even stood in one of the first lines to watch for him in case he walked past us.

While waiting in line, a gentleman next to us had a radio and told me a plane had crashed into the Pentagon. He also heard that one plane (out of the four "known" hijacked planes) had still not been accounted for, and that the FAA had grounded all planes in the US while all international flights were being sent to Canada.

My eyes were killing me from all the dust and soot in the air. I walked over to the "floating hospital boat" and was able to get us (and the gentleman with the radio) surgical masks while we waited in line for the ferry to leave.

(10:15 am – 10:45 am) South Street Seaport

We continued to wait in line for the ferries to start boarding and kept a close watch for Bill. I don't know why, but I felt responsible for us not being able to stay together. I was concerned for Bill because I knew he didn't have an ID, money, credit cards or shoes. Although I kept telling myself how resourceful he was, as his friend, I was upset that he was in this - whatever it was - all alone. I kept flashing back to how scared I had felt when I had gotten off the hotel elevator at the Marriott and thought that I was completely alone. I knew in my mind that during all the side street commotion, he had broken away and taken off towards the bridge; the rest of this journey would be without him.

One thing stands out so vividly in my mind as we waited in line. Even though we could not see one building in front of us, I will never forget the sound that came from the white and black clouds of smoke. Out of nowhere came the solid and evident sound of our military fighter jets. I remember hearing some of the people in line gasping in horror when they heard the sounds. I turned and said, "Those are ours...our fighters...and they are here protecting us now." I almost broke down in tears; they were the sweetest sounds my ears had heard all day.

How did I know these sounds were coming from our fighter jets? I was an F-4E flight line jet engine mechanic in the USAF, 512th TFS, Ramstein AB Germany – so yes, I knew those beautiful sounds!

We finally heard a man asking if anyone else was going to Hoboken in our line because that boat had extra seats. I remember turning to Tina, Bernie and Ragu and saying, "We are going wherever the first ferry out of here is taking us."

I wanted out of the city so badly. We still had no idea what was going on around us.

(10:45 am –11:45 am) South Street Seaport to Hoboken

It wasn't until after we had gotten on the ferry that we heard the towers had collapsed. The ferry ride around the city towards Hoboken showed what I didn't really believe: the Twin Towers were gone. Bellowing smoke was coming from huge, gaping spaces where I had just slept, ran on the treadmill and gotten my first cup of coffee of the day. There wasn't even a ghostly silhouette of where I had just been, only shadows of blackness....

We were still trying to make some sense of all the things we were seeing for the first time. We still had no way of contacting anyone via our cell phones.

Half way to Hoboken, we were detoured to Jersey City because Hoboken had become the emergency route for the injured. It wasn't until we docked in Jersey City that for the first time since 8:45 am, I started to feel a little bit safe again.

(11:45 am – 12:00 pm) Jersey City, NJ

We left and walked towards the crowds of people being directed to an emergency evacuation center. No one could tell us exactly where it was, so when the first bus pulled up and stopped, we all got on and headed towards the Hoboken train station. Our agreed upon strategy was that we would try to get out of the congested areas so we could find ways to get home to our families.

(12:00 pm – 1:00 pm) Hoboken Station, NJ

Once we got to this train station, we all stood in line and waited to use the outside pay phones to contact our loved ones; we wanted to let them know we were alive and trying to get home. I called my husband and tried to coordinate a location where he could meet us. Getting to Newark Penn Station was the objective at this point.

The closest we could get to Newark Penn Station was the Gladstone train station. Everything started to become so chaotic again. I barely had time to buy everyone water and snacks before we were herded onto the trains for security reasons. Then, we ended up switching trains at Hoboken three to four times before we even left. No one knew what was going on.

(1:00 pm – 1:15 pm) Gladstone Station, NJ

When we arrived at this train station, we were told we would need to board another bus that would take us to Newark Penn Station. I remember how new these buses were and that the "new bus smell" was so strong, adding to my existing headache.

(1:15 pm – 2:00 pm) Newark Penn Station, NJ

Everything was so confusing at this train station. My husband could not get close enough to us due to all the congestion and security. Thus, our next step was to get to the Elizabeth train station.

After we tried to get on a train going to Elizabeth train station, we were told we would need to go through a "quarantine process" for asbestos, which meant we were going to be hosed off. We decided to explore other ways of getting out of this area because walking around in wet clothing was nothing short of adding insult to injury, especially after the day we had experienced. "Hosing us down" was not an option.

Shortly afterwards, Ragu was able to find a bus that could take him to Baltimore, MD, which was 60 miles from his home. We said our first goodbyes and wished him a safe journey to his family.

Bernie, Tina and I started walking away from the Newark train station in hopes of finding a cab/taxi/car service that would drive us to the Elizabeth train station. We were fortunate to find a taxi almost immediately. We had to pay big bucks and duck down in the taxi floor to get out of the area since all taxi/cab services were to be used for emergency situations only. (It's always good to carry cash when traveling!)

(2:00 pm – 2:30 pm) Elizabeth Station, NJ

We arrived at this tiny little train station and waited for about a half an hour before my husband arrived to pick us up. Tina called to make arrangements for a rental car, and Bernie called his family to pick him up at a rest area near my house.

(4:15 pm – 4:45 pm) Jersey Shores, NJ

We headed south for the closest place available that was still renting out cars. Tina and I followed my husband and Bernie to a rest area on the NJ Turnpike.

(4:45 pm – 6:00 pm) NJ Turnpike exit (7A)

Tina, Bernie, my husband and I waited at a rest stop off of the NJ Turnpike until Bernie's family arrived. We said goodbye again as Bernie left with his family. Then it was Tina's turn. We hugged and said good-bye.

Wednesday, September 12th, 2001

I spoke with Tina throughout her drive back to her family. I don't think I slept a minute until I knew she was home safely.

Again, we followed through on our "leave no man behind" promise.

My buddy, Bill, was reunited with his family the next day. He had made his way over the Manhattan Bridge after our separation, when we thought car bombs were going off in the streets and didn't realize that the first tower had collapsed. From what I understand, he found refuge in the Brooklyn Marriott overnight. He, too, made it home (a day later) safe and sound.

Although I was extremely fortunate to survive, I will carry many different scars from this experience with me forever.

Crystal Pedone-Cattano

DONNA FOURNIER CUOMO
A former state representative from Massachusetts is separated from her husband

---

Donna Fournier Cuomo, a former state representative from the Greater Boston area, was traveling with her husband to New York on September 11, 2001. The two were hotel guests on the 15th floor of the World Trade Center. Her husband was attending an economics conference in the World Trade Center while Donna was inside the hotel room. They were separated temporarily during the tragic events but were able to unite later. In her escape, Donna suffered some injuries due to tripping over twisted metal. Donna Fournier Cuomo is the founder of a victim support and violence prevention organization named in memory of her brother, who was brutally murdered at the age of seventeen. Through this organization, Donna aims to provide healing for those whose loved ones have been murdered and who witnessed the devastating attacks of 9/11.

"I AM HAUNTED BY THE FACES OF THE PEOPLE WE MET AT THE WORLD TRADE CENTER AS WELL AS THE FIREFIGHTERS AND POLICE OFFICERS WHO HELPED US TO SAFETY. I OFTEN TIMES WONDER IF THEY ARE ALIVE OR DEAD."

ON SEPTEMBER 11, 2001, when the Twin Towers of the World Trade Center (WTC) in New York came crashing down after a terrorist attack of immense proportions, my husband Bob and I narrowly escaped the fire, smoke and debris. Haunted by the memories of the people we met there and who may now be dead, we keep going over the surreal events of that tragic morning.

Bob, who was a principal for an economics consulting firm, was giving a presentation at the National Association for Business Economics on the first floor of the Marriott Hotel located between the WTC Twin Towers.

At 8:48 am, the building shook. Debris began falling from the ceiling and people started running out of the conference room—it was pandemonium.

Bob helped six people who had been trampled by the crowd. No one knew that the first plane, American Airlines Flight 11, had just struck the WTC North Tower. At the same time, I heard a loud noise and something hitting the window of our hotel room on the 15th floor. When I looked out, I saw smoldering papers falling from the sky and fire and smoke billowing out of the North Tower. On the ground, people were racing out of the hotel onto the plaza between the two towers while fire darted all around.

At that point, I had to get down to the lobby as quickly as possible.

As everyone began leaving the hotel, Bob waited frantically for me as droves of people began appearing from the stairwells. The firefighters could not let him go upstairs to find me. Hampered by recent foot surgery, I started struggling down the stairs. A man came up behind me, who I offered to let go ahead. He declined, which helped me move as fast as possible. As the crowds of hotel guests dwindled to a handful, Bob convinced a firefighter to let him climb the stairs.

At just that time, I made it to the top of the staircase that led to the lobby. Little did we know what horror lied ahead—and that the worst of our ordeal was yet to come. A second plane, United Airlines Flight 175, had just hit the WTC South Tower. Due to the falling debris, the Marriott staff told us we couldn't leave the building until the firefighters could escort us out. Several minutes later, we were directed by the firefighters to exit the hotel. Once we were on the street, the firefighters began yelling, "Run! Don't look up! Run!"

Just then, I tripped over a large piece of twisted metal that had fallen. I badly bruised my chin and left foot and cut both knees. Bob quickly helped me up and we continued down the Joe DiMaggio Highway. Along the route were signs of the devastation. We saw a wheel from one of the planes, an abandoned car that had slammed into a storefront and body parts including an arm strewn along the sidewalk.

As we made our escape, shopkeepers, firefighters and police remained behind. When we got a few blocks away, we stopped to catch our breath. People were in shock and questioning whether the South Tower would topple over. After we crossed under the overpass to the Brooklyn Battery Tunnel onto Broadway, suddenly a wave of black smoke and ash engulfed the street. The South Tower had collapsed. People were running for cover.

We went into an office building where the air quality in the lobby soon became very poor. The building security gave masks to everyone and urged people to go up to the offices. I kept thinking we should be going underground. With few options left, we took the elevator to the 18th floor with employees of Fleet Financial Services. Meanwhile, our son Mark and daughter Rachel had watched the news in horror as the South Tower collapsed on what was once the WTC Marriott Hotel. Later, Fleet Financial let us use the telephone to call our son Mark. Within minutes, a second wave of black smoke and ash engulfed the area. The WTC North Tower had just collapsed. It was like an eruption, and the intensity was so great that it affected the air quality on the 18th floor. Since the effects outside were even worse, everyone remained in the building for over two hours before security began allowing people to leave.

Some people decided to take the ferry to New Jersey, while others walked over the Brooklyn and Manhattan Bridges. Bob and I were the last ones to leave, and when we got outside onto the street, the heavy soot, which covered everything, was blowing in our eyes. We used the masks and began walking toward the river.

Very few people were on the streets, however. We met many police officers sent to New York to help with the evacuation. Since the subway was running in some parts of the city, we decided to try to get to Penn Station to get a train to Boston. First, we had to walk to the Lower East Side, making a horseshoe loop along the East River into Chinatown. For what seemed like forever, we walked - past the Brooklyn and Manhattan Bridges until we reached a working subway station. With few options, we took the subway and continued onto Penn Station.

Upon arriving at Penn Station at 4:30 pm, we found that all the shops were closed as well as the Amtrak ticket booths. Two personnel at an information counter said an Acela train was due to arrive from Washington D.C. It was delayed, and they didn't know when it would be here. They said we wouldn't need a ticket to board. At 5:45 pm, almost without warning, they announced the arrival of the Acela train. Eventually, we all were allowed to board, and finally at 6:00 pm, the train pulled out of New York City for Boston. At one point as the train moved away, everyone looked out the window to see the smoldering fire and smoke of the WTC in the distance. It was hard to imagine that a few hours earlier we were at the WTC with thousands of others who were alive and well, going to work, but now were dead. The train continued on to South Station where our family was there to meet us, so relieved and grateful we had survived this ordeal.

In the days following September 11th, I have gone over the events in my mind. I am haunted by the faces of the people we met at the WTC as well as the firefighters and police officers who helped us to safety. I often times wonder if they are alive or dead. Feelings of anger at the terrorists and sadness for the thousands of victims who lost their lives remain immense. Concern for the families of the victims comes from knowing first-hand what it means when someone you love is murdered. In 1974, my seventeen year-old brother Joey, a high school student, was murdered while working part-time at a gas station in Lawrence. For each murder victim, there are several homicide survivors left behind - someone's child, mother, father, wife, husband, brother or sister. The shock, anger and indescribable grief that each survivor will endure is overwhelming. It is a challenge to us all to meet the needs of the families and help ease the pain of those survivors who live in Massachusetts. To meet this challenge will require a resolve and sense of purpose that is unprecedented.

FATHER PAUL ENGEL

*A 64 year-old priest escapes death
by seconds in the hotel gym*

---

*Father Paul Engel was about to go swimming at the World Trade
Center Hotel gym on the 22nd floor. He had just changed into
swim clothes when the landing gear from the first plane crashed
into the roof of the hotel. As a result, the hotel caught on fire and
the pool went up in flames.*

"IT SOUNDED LIKE SOMETHING FELL OUT OF THE
SKY. I WAS THINKING SOME KIND OF ASTRONOMICAL
THING FELL ON THE HOTEL. IT SHOOK THE WHOLE
BUILDING – AND A BUILDING LIKE THAT DOESN'T
SHAKE. THE WHOLE SWIMMING POOL WAS ON FIRE,
THE WATER WAS ON FIRE."

I am a victim of 9/11.

ON THE DAY of 9/11, I was working out in the gym. The gym was on the 22nd floor of the hotel that connected the two towers. It was filled with all types of workout machines where people were exercising. Over the pool was a glass dome that let light in.

It was a beautiful day. I did my work out on the exercise bike.

Next, I was going to do my laps in our swimming pool because there was nobody in it. It was a small pool, probably one of the smallest pools that you could fit in. Just before I dove in, I decided that I was not going to swim. I no sooner left the pool area and headed to the men's changing rooms when everything went **boom!** The lights went out and the loud speaker went on, telling everybody to get out of the building.

I didn't know what I thought I was thinking. It sounded like something fell out of the sky. I was thinking some kind of astronomical thing fell on the hotel. It shook the building – and a building like that doesn't shake. The hotel was between the two towers. We were on the top floor, the 22nd floor in the gym.

I followed the instructions from the intercom. When I ran out the men's locker room, I put a towel over me. We were really scared. The whole swimming pool was on fire - even the water was covered in flames. I guess what happened, as I was told, was that one of the motors on the rig of the first plane torpedoed through the skylight roof over the pool, which I had very nearly jumped into minutes before. I guess in a way, Mr. Death didn't get me that day, so I was very fortunate.

What I remember - although I remember very little from that occasion - is running down the stairs to get out of the hotel. The debris looked like confetti.

When I got down to the bottom, nobody knew what was going on. Somebody said that a small plane had crashed into the tower. We now know it was not a small plane.

I was running and I cut my feet since I wasn't wearing shoes. I ran out of the building then fell down underneath the passage way that went from the hotel to the other side of the West Side Highway. A policeman and a fireman picked me up and carried me across the street. When I looked up, I saw the second plane hit the South Tower.

The firefighter and police officer carried me up to the top of Battery Park, where my apartment was located. Some residents noticed me bleeding and told me to get inside. As soon I got up there, they said we had to leave the apartment.

That whole day was incredible. When I came back out of my building, I was approached by a young man in a wheelchair. He was bleeding badly, so I gave him the sacrament of mixed emotion: I bent over and prayed with him. Suddenly, a police officer was telling us that we had to leave the area. We began walking towards the West Side Highway and witnessed the two towers going down.

I couldn't believe what I was looking at. It was just crazy; everything stopped. There were no taxis. There were no cars. Everything just stopped in the city. I'll never forget that experience. Somebody said I was running with other people. They wanted me to go with them to New Jersey on a boat, but I said no. I wanted to stay there, so I went up to my office on 34th Street. I managed to find refuge at a hotel near my office and get some sleep.

Over the course of that day, my family didn't know what had happened to me. The whole time they had been trying to reach me, stricken with fear of the unknown.

Eventually, I went into therapy for almost two years after the incident. Most of what came out of my therapy was a feeling of guilt. We lost so many people - in fact 3,000 - and we watched it all happen. I felt so guilty that I was spared, but also that there was a purpose to my survival. As a priest working with homeless kids, I was now even more confident that this is was what God wanted me to do with my life. He wanted me to stay alive and continue my mission.

Many of the employees of Cantor Fitzgerald, an office that lost almost all of its staff on 9/11, have been extremely supportive of my cause. Every year, they raise money for the children. Their generosity reminds me of their own suffering - so many of them were killed that day. This realization has made me even more determined to pursue my mission for homeless kids.

9/11 was a tragic experience, and I don't think I'll ever get over it.

At the time, I was so angry. I was asking myself, "Why did they do this to us?" But I've come a long way since then. I pray for the terrorists now. I'm sorry they were so determined to do what they did.

So many families I know lost loved ones. They'll never get over it. Some were young people just starting out their lives. Some had small children, who will now never know their mothers or fathers. We even heard of one family with a few of kids who lost both their parents. They'll never recover from that loss. This is all just tragic.

For years, I had a hard time going into public places because if I felt or heard noise, my blood pressure would go up. I've never really gotten over the noise. I've never really gotten over the feelings. They bring back the horrible memories of 9/11. They traumatize me even to this day.

I feel so blessed that I survived.

MICHAEL R. ENGLUND

A minute to minute account of the horror

Michael R. Englund is Principal Director and Chief Economist of Action Economics. On September 11, 2001, he was attending the NABE annual economics conference in the hotel's conference room. He remembers in excruciating detail all the events from September 11th and narrates each incident, sensation and thoughts from that day.

"RIGHT IN FRONT OF THE HOTEL WAS A BUS THAT WAS PARTIALLY CRUSHED IN ITS MIDDLE BY A BUILDING PART, AND THE DRIVER WAS STANDING, DAZED, NEXT TO HIS BUS WITH HIS HANDS REACHING OUT. PEOPLE COULD BE HEARD OUTSIDE SCREAMING AND CRYING, EVEN THROUGH THE WINDOWS OF THE HOTEL."

Brevity is lost on 9/11

GENERALLY, I LIKE to think that I prefer brevity, but I thought it would be worth recording the event in detail here and leave it to the reader to skim, or for me to edit it down at some time in the future to a tolerable length for my own purposes. Here, I simply tried to record all the images and thoughts that I was experiencing, moment by moment. I left out much of the detail about my own personal thoughts, which would obviously make this story even longer! I limited what I wrote here to the facts as I experienced them. As such, I guess I am not just apologizing for the excessive length, but also for the lack of any personal thoughts about friends and family that obviously were on my mind at the time, but that I chose not to record here for posterity.

The morning of September 11ᵗʰ

On September 11, I was attending a NABE conference at the World Trade Center with roughly 300 other economists. About half of the conference participants, including myself, attended a breakfast meeting with the CEO of Morgan Stanley starting around 8:00 that morning, in the first floor conference room of the Marriott World Trade Center. The hotel was adjacent to both the North and South towers, in the southwest corner of the WTC complex. The parking lot below the hotel, which was previously called the Vista, was the site of the 1993 World Trade Center bombing.

The hotel conference room

The conference room was typical of such conferences, with a couple of large double doors at the entrance of a huge square room, and a high 30-35 foot ceiling. Also as is typical of conference rooms, the ceiling lights were configured to appear like an enormous chandelier, though this "chandelier" was really a huge array of hundreds of individual small glass tubes with bulbs between them, each suspended by a separate wire from the ceiling. The entire array of ceiling lights was probably about 60 feet long and 30 feet wide.

The morning breakfast meeting started like any other conference session, and the speaker had just started his remarks when, at 8:46, the audience became aware that something was happening in the building.

Harmonic frequency of the unlit bulbs

The slow passage of a broad black "band" of temporarily unlit bulbs passed from the east end of the conference room chandelier to the west end, and it took several seconds to completely cross the room. The pattern was similar to the slow passage of a black band on a TV set when the vertical hold is slightly out of whack. Many of us looked at each other when this started, and the "scientifically minded" were probably thinking about what sort of "harmonic frequency" disturbance might cause this strange pattern in the electrical system.

Tinkling sounds

This pattern was quickly followed by the "tinkling" sound of the individual glass tubes hitting each other. Many of us looked at each other again, but more worried this time, as this indicated that it was a "physical" shock that was impacting the building rather than an electrical shock. Though somewhat worried, most participants acted at first as if the strange shock was over, and the speaker kept talking through the episode.

But before the tinkling sound stopped, and probably within three or four seconds of the first distraction, a series of crashing and screeching sounds started that seemed to be coming from the floor immediately above. These sounds were what you would expect if a bunch of conference room tables that had been folded up and set against each other tipped over, and crashed onto the floor one at a time, with assorted scraping metal causing the screeching. The sound was loud enough to cause the speaker to stop talking, but not loud enough, at that point, to prompt panic. In fact, it seemed for a second that the sounds had stopped, and that the speaker would try to say something lighthearted to re-focus the room.

Banging sounds

But then—and this was about six seconds into the event—the sounds took a nasty turn. First there was a string of banging sounds that were much louder and deeper than the ones before, and that had the resonance of a huge catastrophe rather than falling furniture. Underlying the loud banging sound was an escalating roar, that also resonated with the building, and that you could feel through your feet and chair, as well as hear.

The sounds may not have been as loud as I remember them, but my experience was colored by my interpretation of what was happening. The earlier sounds seemed like something you often hear in a building, so the natural instinct was to "explain it away." But the later roar had a ferocity and depth that was at odds with normal experience, and this likely made the noise seem much louder, and more horrific.

My guess is that others actually shared my series of very specific, and partly inaccurate, thoughts at that time. I immediately recalled the 1993 World Trade Center bombing, as I often did when I entered the Marriott hotel. My first thought was that Terrorists had set off a similar bomb at the bottom of one of the two towers, and that the horrible roar was the collapse of one of the towers. When I pictured the imaginary collapse in my mind, I felt it would probably take five or ten seconds for the top of the building to reach the ground, and I therefore sensed that I had just a few seconds left to "do something" before the building we were in collapsed with it.

My first feelings of doom

It was only then that I realized the stampede around me, as others were quicker at assessing the risk of being in the middle of a huge conference room with few structural supports in a collapsing building. The immediate sensation was that we were doomed, as the ceiling seemed enormous, while the doors appeared tiny in proportion. I started to run with everyone else, but was well aware that I would never make it through the doors before the building collapsed. I considered jumping under a table, but they were far to flimsy to be helpful. I focused on the ceiling, with the assumption that I could dodge debris.

By the time I made it to the doors of the conference room, the roaring sound was subsiding, and was being replaced by the diverging "tones" of dozens of voices. Some voices sounded hysterical, while others were growing more determined. Most people were quiet and watchful, as they looked around for leads. My own sensation was of relief that the building had not collapsed, and that there was a remote chance that the whole disturbance would prove to be substantially less horrible than feared. Nevertheless, the crowd continued to scramble, and I found myself telling people to slow down, as a few people closer to the front of the mob had fallen, and appeared at risk of being trampled by the people behind them. In total, the scene as we left the conference room mostly reflected a diminishing degree of panic, but with some people clearly becoming more agitated, and everyone becoming increasingly convinced by the breadth of confusion in the hallway that a sizable calamity at some location near us was underway.

It was noteworthy with hindsight that our crowd veered left, into the lobby of the Marriott Hotel, and not right, into the lobby of the North Tower. Whereas the hotel lobby revealed no physical damage within the building, and only small windows through which to assess the crisis outside, the lobby of the North Tower experienced a fireball of burning fuel, and large windows through which the falling debris and fire would have been clearly visible. Without knowing it, our meeting participants made a fortunate decision in running into the hotel.

The hotel lobby

Upon reaching the lobby, the panic was replaced by disbelief, as the crowd strained to look out the window into the surreal landscape of crisis surrounded the building. Building parts were everywhere, and chunks continued hitting the ground with loud, powerful thuds. All the traffic on the West Side Highway was at a complete standstill, which was itself an extraordinary sight for downtown. Several cars were crushed by debris, and several small fires were visible, as well as smoking objects. Right in front of the hotel was a bus that was partially crush in its middle by a building part, and the driver was standing, dazed, next to his bus with his hands reaching out. People could be heard outside screaming and crying, even through the windows of the hotel.

Was it dangerous to leave?

The first thought was that it would be dangerous to leave the hotel, given the continuous stream of large objects audibly crashing into the ground about once every five to ten seconds. The crowd mulled for direction, and

I had conversations with quite a few people. Finally, I told one individual that I was going to leave the building through a smaller south-side exit that I knew of, and not wait for any sort of "official notification." About a dozen of the people in the lobby went with me.

When I got to the south-side revolving door there was no-one there, so I went partially through the door to the outside portion where I stopped to look up for falling debris. Amazingly, it was impossible to tell if any large objects were falling, despite the fact that it was a perfectly clear day. The sky was peppered with millions of pieces of paper that were falling and swaying in the wind, as in a ticker-tape parade. The objects blocked the capacity to focus on any particular item, so it was clear that the exit strategy would be a straight and rapid run across the street, and beyond the apparent impact zone, with no chance that anyone could successfully "dodge" falling objects. Though it was still not possible to see what had happened, it was at least now clear that some kind of bomb had exploded in the building above, and it was also now substantially less clear that the best strategy was to make a "run for it" across the street.

This new decision point was brought to a quick close, however, when a young police officer ran toward me from the south side of the street with a very confused and terrified look on his face, while yelling that I should leave the building while focusing his attention on the tower above. My first thought was that he may know something that I didn't, and that this was why he was so willing to have me take my chances with the falling objects rather than stay in the building. It then suddenly occurred to me that the dozen people behind me were stuck inside the revolving door unless I left, so the decision to leave had effectively been made for me by circumstance. Somewhat relieved that I didn't have to fully assess this new situation myself, I put my hand over my head and ran to a place under a "skyway" to the southwest of the building that connected downtown with Battery Park City" on the west side of Manhattan. I then ran across the West Side Hi-way underneath the skyway, while looking up at the building over my shoulder for the first time to see the huge hole that is now widely familiar to everyone. When I crossed the highway I felt safe from debris, and was finally able to detach myself from my "crisis management" mindset.

The call home

At this point, it was clear to me that I had to call my wife at once, as she always watched TV in the morning, and clearly the sight I was seeing would be the image on virtually every channel. Fortunately, the chaos of people in the streets—who were displaying the full range of human emotion and were quite vocal—did not include many who were looking for a phone. I was quite familiar with Battery Park City because I had spent many occasions staying there in a company apartment, so I knew where I could find a phone about two blocks from the Towers. When I got there the phone was available, and I was able to call Melissa and tell her I was safe, and that I would call her later in the day when I had a chance. I asked her to call our office in Belmont, so they would all know that I had gotten out of the building. I had no idea that this would be my last chance to call out for quite a while given the problems that soon emerged with most of the phones in the city, and that most of the horrors of the crisis were still to be seen.

On my way to the phone, I participated in about a dozen separate conversations with random store owners, commuters, and tourists, who were sharing information in the sidewalk to help everyone assess the situation. Some people who were eye witnesses of the impact, and who were also generally the most agitated people on the sidewalk, were yelling that it was a cruise missile or some kind of military jet, and that the city was under attack. Store keepers and others who seemed to have come out of some of the small shops, and who had not directly witnessed the impact, were saying that it was a small plane—not a missile—and that it seemed to be some kind of aviation mistake. Most people were simply focused on the huge hole and fire, and were talking or crying about the fate of the people inside.

The sidewalk talk

These conversations with passers-by continued after I hung up, though the tone became decisively worse. As I started walking back toward the building to make some kind of decision about where to go next, the "sidewalk talk" was that it was actually a very large plane and not a small one. Though no-one talked about the fire in specific while I was searching for the phone, the sense I had was that most people expected it to be put out, and to visibly diminish in size fairly quickly. On the way back though, the fire was growing bigger, and people were talking more about the fire itself. The sense of crisis in the streets was getting worse. As I got back toward the skyway, people started to yell "jumpers" and the crowd broke into screams and cries for help. Though some people were looking up at the building, pointing, and holding their mouths, others were buckling over, or turning away crying. I looked up and saw a stream of several people jumping, and quickly chose to look away myself. The flow of jumpers seemed to continue from then on, and it became hard to look up at the building.

I then noticed that the police were putting up yellow tape around the building, and the tape was starting to cut me off from the rest of Manhattan where I would likely want to go next. As I started jogging back toward the building to "beat the tape," I quickly decided that I would return to my Standard & Poor's office at 55 Water Street, where I could tell my colleagues in New York what had happened, and where I could also use the phone to call home again.

The other plane

My timing wasn't good. I passed about two or three blocks straight south of the South Tower at 9:03, where I was walking south and continuing to have conversations with people I passed on the sidewalk about the situation. At one point I started to realize that we were all talking increasingly loudly to shout above a mounting roar that was adding to the sounds of the flaming building and screamers on the sidewalks. Suddenly, a man in front of me looked up and yelled "it's another plane," at which point everyone on the street broke into a run away from the building.

I never saw the plane. But as I looked over my shoulder at the roar that I was now suddenly focused on, all I saw was an exploding fireball that reached from the building to a point almost directly above me, with flying debris that covered a vast expanse of the sky, and that made me and my small city block seem puny. The illusion was that the Tower was falling on me like a huge tree, and that my running was laughably futile. In my mind, the image of the building grew vaster than it had ever appeared when I was walking around the streets of New York, or on the many client-visits that

I had made to the various floors inside the Towers. The vast arrays of cubicles and trading desks on every floor now seemed even more extraordinary in volume and number. It seemed to me that this collapsing "tree" would crush all the buildings around me, that it would crash through the pavement and deep into the earth, and that the sheer concussion effect would topple buildings around the crash. I was almost certainly going to die in about six seconds.

Though confused by these thoughts, I also had a sense that maybe it wasn't really happening. That maybe, at least, the building wasn't really falling and that if I jumped under something big I would survive. There was a doorway to the right where a glass door was open, and it was in the ground floor of another tall building that appeared to constitute a viable shield. I veered right into the doorway and into some kind of workout facility, again followed by a spattering of people. As if the protection of the building wasn't enough, I dove onto the ground between an array of Stairmasters. In the back of my mind, I dwelled on this last, silly, ignorant act—puzzled why I would think that the Tower would crash through a few dozen floors of the building above me, but would be stopped by an array of workout equipment. I wondered if there was one last thing I could do to improve my chances, and I started to wonder when the building would hit the ground.

Instead of the horrible crash I had expected, I heard a splash of glass and metal objects slamming into the streets around the building. I never felt the "concussion" that I was braced for. With a few seconds pause, I realized that the building had not fallen, though I wasn't sure what to expect outside. I stood up but stayed between the Stairmasters, on the assumption that a building collapse remained a possibility even if it hadn't occurred yet. A guy near the window got up, looked out the window, and said that there was another huge hole in the Tower. This actually seemed like good news, as it implied that the building was still standing and looked "stable." I decided to get out of the area, and consider myself lucky that my sudden imaginary brush with death was now behind me.

Debris everywhere

The street was now littered with building debris, and the obvious conclusion that this was a terrorist attack that could be repeated seemed quite clear to everyone around me. I ran slowly but deliberately through the city blocks in a zig-zag pattern so that I could put buildings between me and the Towers in a diagonal pattern that would provide protection if the building was to fall sideways. With hindsight, I realize that a collapse would be "downward" and not "sideways," but this was not the intuitive sense I had from the perspective of the street. My route took me straight to work, where I was anxious to see my colleagues and tell them what had happened, as well as to call my family again.

The tone in the streets changed as I put distance between myself and the building. The people near the building at the time of the second strike clearly perceived themselves to be "inside" the crisis, and escape was their goal. The flow of foot traffic was decisively away from the building. By about the fifth or sixth block, the traffic pattern was random, and the majority of people were more grief-stricken than scared. These people did not perceive themselves to be in personal physical danger, but were focused on friends or family that worked closer to, or in, the building. By the eighth block, the flow of foot traffic was toward the building.

Finding my colleague, John

When I reached 55 Water Street, there was a huge collection of employees in the lobby, so I started to wonder if I should look for colleagues there rather than going up to the office. A security guard announced that people should return to work, though the flow of people up the elevators and down was relatively balanced. I ended up finding John, a longtime colleague—in the lobby, and the two of us discussed a plan, including my own personal plan. Only now was I beginning to realize that I may not be going back to my hotel room at the Marriott later that day, and that my only belongings were now the suit I was wearing, my wallet, and my NABE name tag. John offered that I could go home with him that evening, and probably unknowingly committed himself to what turned out to be my three night stay with his wife and son in Queens. Since the Tower had not earlier collapsed, I strangely re-adopted my earlier assumption that the fire would eventually be put out. My assumption at that point was that my inability to return to my hotel room would be because of police barricades blocking the building for some period of time, and not the reality that the hotel would collapse soon after the two towers.

John and I decided to return to our office on the 46th floor to tell all the analysts that we should all go home for the day, and to make sure that no-one felt compelled to stay at work. We reached our own "trading floor" around 9:40, and immediately began talking to the cluster of analysts that were at the windows, through which we had a painfully clear view of what was happening at the Twin Towers. I was running through my experience with them, and we started to compare notes on what the inside of the Towers was like, and how the people above the two burning holes in the building were likely getting past the fires on their way down.

The South tower falls

Right at that point, which was apparently 9:50, I started to notice that the South Tower seemed to be moving, and within an instant everyone on our floor was gasping as we realized that this enormous building was about to collapse to the ground right in front of us. Someone yelled "get back from the windows," and I suspect others shared my fear that the collapse would send such a powerful shock through Manhattan that other buildings would be shaken. One employee grabbed a rope to close the blinds, though our windows stretched across the entire length of the building, so this act was pointless. I yelled to run toward the center of the building, and I ran to an interior room near the elevator shaft, which I thought would be the safest place to be if the building absorbed a jolt, and parts of the building, or the glass, gave way.

As is it was, there was no jolt, and I quickly ran back to the window to see what had happened. Indeed, there was only one tower remaining, and all of downtown below the 15th-20th floor seemed to be gobbled up by an enormous "upside down" mushroom cloud that had engulfed lower Manhattan and was broadening rapidly to absorb Brooklyn.

It was immediately clear that we were now all going to leave, and everyone started to talk about whether they could avoid breathing in the cloud that they could see below. John said that he was going right away, and again invited me to drive back to his house in his car. All the analysts, John, and myself left the building.

The cloud of dust

I walked with John back to his car, and the air was actually quite clear given that the wind was blowing toward the east and we were south of the Towers. As we got to his car, however, we were starting to enter the "cloud," and it started to become hard to breathe or see clearly. John's car was a convertible, and we drove through the heart of the cloud in a mild north-bound traffic jam, alongside an enormous foot-based exodus around us. Most people looked like us, with a light covering of white dust over business suits, maintaining a steady but deliberate pace to the north. But at any time you could see at least one or two people that were heavily doused in white dust, and there was a continuous peppering of people in the crowd that were limping, yelling, crying, or running. At one point in this exodus we heard a powerful rumbling sound, and it was clear to John and me that this was the sound of the second tower falling.

We eventually made it past the downtown area and started heading at a more rapid clip northbound on the East Side Highway to leave Manhattan, though we were aware from the news on the radio that the bridges were closed. John parked his car in a place where we could easily enter a bridge entrance ramp when it opened, and we left the car in search of a phone. We tried several different phones, and made repeated attempts at a call, before we finally got a "line out," so we could tell people what had happened. I again called my wife to give her the "short version" of this story, and asked her to call others and let them know that I was O.K., as were my colleagues. She was quite relieved at the call, given the coverage she was seeing on TV. And the people in our Belmont office were particularly relieved given that they had little contact with any of the analysts in New York through the crisis, and really didn't know what was happening to anyone. Of all places, John and I then went to a bar(!), where we had a beer and watched the TV news for updates. We soon read on the scrolling news that the bridges were re-opening. We quickly went back to the car and drove in surprisingly little traffic up the on ramp and across the bridge, with a brief stop to pick up a hitch hiker.

There is really no natural end to this disaster story, and the events that followed were in some ways as surreal and as difficult to grasp as the attack itself.

Three days to get home to Colorado

It took three days for me to find a flight home to Boulder, which I spent with John and his family. We all re-lived the events and discussed what was still happening around us, and what was likely to happen in the world going forward. We had conference calls with colleagues to discuss our policies at work and, of all things, our economic outlook. I had repeated opportunities to call home and talk with my wife, kids, and parents, to discuss what had happened and reassure them that I was O.K. My home, meanwhile, became a little "media" center, as my name appeared in some Standard & Poor's news report somewhere, and the press immediately surrounded Melissa in search of TV and newsprint interviews.

It was a great joy when I was finally able to get a flight home from Newark and reunite with my family. The memories will always remain, but going home at least brought my own physical parameters of this unbelievable disaster to a close.

JOAN FILSON

A woman humbled by the kindness shown on 9/11

Joan Filson was attending an economics conference at the Marriott World Trade Center hotel. At the time of the attack, she was in the Grand Ballroom on the ground floor of the hotel, listening to the morning speakers address the group. She was staying on the 14th floor of the hotel.

"A THICK CLOUD OF SMOKE COVERED US AND IT WAS HARD TO BREATHE."

M Y 9/11 STORY begins the day before the attacks on Monday, September 10. I was in the middle of the National Association for Business Economics' annual meeting entitled, "NABE in a New York Minute: in the Midst of Economic Uncertainty" at the Hotel in the World Trade Center:

After a press visit to the NYSE, our incoming president and I walked back to the World Trade Center to the hotel. It rained suddenly and we took shelter under an awning.

"If this is the worst thing that happens, it's been a great meeting," he said.

An eerie irony

That evening, a reporter friend and I made a late-night visit to Windows on the World, the famous restaurant atop the North Tower. We had to do it that night - our conference was scheduled to end at 2:30 pm on September 11, the next day. The hotel and the towers were interconnected, making it a short walk to the elevator leading to Windows on the 107th floor. There was an elevator operator to whom we had to display our conference badges. Mid-way up to the 107th floor, we switched elevators. It was a creaky ascent, not something I would want to do every day if I worked in the building. Being that high up, I recalled the 1993 WTC bombings, when a truck bomb exploded beneath the North Tower, killing six people and injuring more than a thousand.

Once at Windows on the World, we walked around the bar, stepped outside on the balcony, admired the night view and peered down. It was inconceivable to us that by mid-morning Tuesday, people would be jumping from here to escape the inferno. We left and took the elevator back to ground level. Later, I would think that we were among the last people to leave Windows on the World alive.

"This is Terrorism"

Tuesday, September 11, was a bright, hot and sunny day – the last day of the NABE annual meeting. It had been a great conference, with more than 250 leading economists in attendance.

On Monday, September 10, the president had presented the NABE Economic Outlook, a quarterly survey of professional macroeconomic forecasters. Respondents were optimistic that recovery from a slowdown was likely by the end of the year. The survey became an important measure of where the economy stood on the eve of the attacks. On Tuesday September 11, many major economists of the country were scheduled to speak, followed by afternoon sessions on demographics and globalization and a visit to the New York Federal Reserve.

Scott was speaking at a breakfast meeting when the first plane hit the North Tower. We were in the Grand Ballroom of the Marriott WTC hotel on the ground level at the base of the North Tower. It felt like an earthquake. The chandeliers shuddered and the lights went out but came back on almost immediately. I looked across the table at our group leader and saw what was apparent to everyone in the room: something was terribly wrong.

Most people jumped up from their chairs and headed for the exits. A large crowd gathered in the hotel lobby. There was uncertainty: *Should we leave the building - as pieces of concrete were starting to fall in front of the hotel - or were we safer staying put?* Someone stopped us from using the front entrance because it seemed dangerous, but the side door in the Tall Ships restaurant was locked, so we went back to the front and walked out.

Police stopped traffic to let the swarms of people cross the busy West Side highway. I walked toward the Hudson River and met a group of NABE delegates. No one knew what had happened. *Did a small plane hit the North Tower? Was there a gas explosion?*

Some wondered if we might be able to resume our sessions in the afternoon, given that the black smoke at the upper levels of the tower appeared to be thinning. But it was hard to ignore the danger. Sharp eyes saw what I missed: bodies, not concrete debris, were falling from the tower. People were jumping to certain death on the ground. Then, I saw the second plane hit the South Tower. As I remember, a chorus of voices sounded the alarm: "this is terrorism." It was time to get out of there.

An ominous sky

I started running south alongside the river and stopped by a group listening to a radio. Rumors were flying: there were seven rogue planes, two of them hovering over Dulles airport...or was it Dallas?

"We have to worry about what's in those planes," someone said. *Deadly bacteria? Poison gas?*

Further on, I joined a NABE group that included officers and students. I will never forget their leadership and kindness. Most cellphones didn't work, but Diane's and Tim's did. They shared their phones. Diane reached her office, where co-workers watching events on TV told us what was happening. Diane asked them to call our families. My future son-in-law took the call at my husband's office in Washington.

"Joan's ok," they told him.

It was six or seven hours before I spoke to my husband from a safe spot in Philadelphia.

I parted from my group when they decided to walk Uptown. I felt safer close to the water, where I was confident that I could swim to New Jersey if I had to. After all, my daughter was to be married in four days in Washington and I had to get home!

I found myself in Battery Park near the tip of Manhattan in the middle of an anxious crowd milling about. People were walking on a ledge by the river, clinging to the metal fence and trying to bypass the throng.

A thick cloud of smoke covered us and it was hard to breathe. Young men, stripped to the waist, volunteered to dip people's shirts in the water so they could breathe through the moisture. My boiled wool jacket, necessary to keep me warm in the air-conditioned hotel, became a gas mask! I was surrounded by strangers, so I tapped people on the shoulder and asked how they were doing. One man lived nearby and was concerned about his dog.

"Do you think my dog will be ok?" he asked.

I wondered when the smoke would lift; a man next to me said it would take at least 48 hours to clear.

Saving grace

When the second tower collapsed, I heard someone say, "Oh my God, here comes a stampede." That was the only time I thought there was a possibility that I could die. But the stampede didn't materialize, the smoke cleared and miracle of miracles, a New York Waterways ferry appeared. It was so close, I could touch it! The same young men who had urged calm helped us over the iron railing and onto the ferry.

Would we would be sitting ducks once waterborne? It didn't matter—it was critical to get out of Manhattan. Getting onto the boat was orderly and the captain told us to put on life vests, as if this were a normal ferry ride across the river. Our rescue boat sped across the water and we were in Jersey City in no time.

I walked off the boat onto the pier probably around noon. There were no buses or organized evacuation efforts at that time. We were on our own. I didn't see anyone I knew, so I spoke to a young woman who was looking across the river at the inferno. She was a student who normally temped at the WTC but had overslept that morning.

She took me to her apartment, where I was finally able to reach my daughter. The young woman knew of a car rental agency, so we walked there and waited two or three hours in a long line of survivors. There was plenty of time to share stories and provide proof, as if it were needed, that we were survivors.

"You don't have any dust on your shoes," said a woman looking at my feet. "Were you really there?"

Thanks to the manager of the Rent-A-Car at Newport Mall, who was working by himself that day, cars and/or rides were found for nearly everyone in line. I shared a car with a group of young traders and interns heading to Philadelphia.

We stopped to get gas ($1.45/gallon) before leaving. The attendant said the New Jersey Turnpike was closed.

"We've got police and emergency crews stopping here to fill up and we know what's going on," he said.

It didn't look closed, so we tried to get on, but police stopped us and said to take US 1 and 9 and get back on the Turnpike at exit 11. It worked! In Philadelphia, the daughter of family friends picked me up and took me to their home, where I spent the night. The next day, I was on the Amtrak home to Washington.

Life lessons learned

I will never forget the competence, kindness and calm determination of everyone I met on my WTC odyssey: my resourceful NABE colleagues, whose leadership and heroic actions continue to inspire me, especially their efforts to track down everyone associated with the meeting to make sure they were ok; the reporters at our conference who transitioned seamlessly from covering economics one minute to war the next; the frightened vendors, still selling water and snacks in Battery Park before the South Tower collapsed; the streams of anxious survivors who helped one another and did not panic; and the New York Waterways and Rent-A-Car staff who helped everyone get home.

I still collect WTC memorabilia. I keep a haunting flyer distributed at the September 11 Marriott Survivors Group 5th anniversary luncheon asking for help in locating a missing person, who was last seen at a department store across from the WTC at 7:13 am on September 10, 2001. My other mementoes - many of which were found in thrift shops - include a small clear-glass replica of the Twin Towers, a painting of the cemetery at St. Paul's Chapel ("the Little Chapel that Stood") with the Twin Towers leaning in like weeping willows, a poster featuring dramatic 9/11 photos on the front pages of newspapers from around the world, and my favorite "Dancin' City" wood pull toy featuring New York's famous buildings, including the Twin Towers.

GREGORY FREDERICK

*The quick thinking of a hotel employee
saves the life of a disabled woman*

Gregory Frederick was a hotel employee working at the Marriot hotel the morning of the 9/11 terrorist attacks. His thoughtfulness and quick actions saved the life of a wheel-chair bound woman with multiple sclerosis. She and her mom were trapped on the fifth floor of the hotel, pleading for help in the hallway as other guests fled. Greg remembered the disabled woman, returned back to check on her and ended up bringing her down using the freight elevators. She and her mother lived because of Greg's heroic actions. It wasn't until eight years later that Greg was able to find the woman and reunite with her in Chicago.

"SOMETIMES OUR CALLING IS WAY BEYOND US, AND THAT'S WHAT HAPPENED TO ME. I HAPPENED TO BE AT THE RIGHT PLACE. I DON'T KNOW WHAT MADE ME THINK ABOUT LEIGH AND FAYE. BUT I THOUGHT ABOUT THEM....I HAD TO GO AND CHECK TO MAKE SURE THAT THEY WERE OK."

I T STARTED LIKE any normal day of work. We were all getting ready to do our duties for the day. Every morning we had a briefing for where we were going to be, a daily agenda for the day.

This particular morning was a little longer than usual because one particular guest, Leigh, was in a wheelchair. Her mother, Faye, had contacted Ponce, the chief building engineer, to fix the bar in the shower. Ponce had briefed us about Leigh being physically challenged and told everyone to pay special attention to these guests due to Leigh's circumstances. After the meeting, I went to Ponce and told him that I would go check their room to make sure that everything was in tip-top shape. I also made sure that everything was according to Leigh's standards to make her happy. We all departed from the meeting and went to our work stations.

The attack on the World Trade Center

That's when all hell broke loose. We heard a big bang and then the alarms from the fire command station went off. Immediately, we all knew to evacuate when we hear that alarm.

All the engineers went directly to the lobby to the fire command station to determine where the fire could possibly be. The panel was totally blown out; you couldn't see anything, you couldn't hear anything; all you heard was the alarms. We saw people running as chaos broke out. We tried to direct all of the guests that were in the lobby to exit the building. Prior to that, all of the elevators had automatically shut down because of the fire alarm. Access to any elevator was now automatically terminated.

We basically mingled around the lobby, trying to get the panel to work. We needed to figure out where the fire had occurred. I was in the lobby for another 15 to 20 minutes - but I can't really say how long it was with all of the confusion happening. I told my manger that I was thinking about the lady on the fifth floor. I didn't know her name. I went directly to her room because us engineers have access to all of the elevators; we can shut them down or bring them up. We also have access to the freight elevators when the guest elevators automatically shut down.

The Rescue of Leigh and Faye

I went up, thinking about Leigh and Faye. Along the way, I saw a lady coming from the revolving door that goes to the Windows of the World. The lady in question was a lady that was later featured in a Ground Zero documentary. She was the lady that was severely burned. She was walking through the lobby confused and badly burned. I looked at her and hollered in shock. I knew that this was bad, that something was bad.

Somebody grabbed her and immediately wrapped a towel – or possibly a tablecloth – around her. They wrapped it around her and exited her out of the building.

I said to myself, "Oh God, this is not good."

I got back to the lobby and remembered the woman that was in the wheelchair. I was still thinking about Faye and Leigh and whether they were ok. So, I immediately took the freight elevator to the fifth floor to check on them.

Although I didn't know their exact room number, I remembered the floor and general location of their room.

I immediately opened the door. To my surprise, Faye and Leigh, as well as another lady whose name I still don't know, were in the room. I asked them what they were still doing up there. They said that they were trapped. Leigh was in her wheelchair, and her mom refused to leave without her.

They couldn't get downstairs because of the wheelchair, and the guest elevators had stopped. I told them that everything was going to be okay; I was here to escort them downstairs using the freight elevator. I want you to come with me please.

I helped Leigh first, as she was in the wheelchair. Faye followed me. The other woman appeared very frightened. She ran back to her room and locked the door.

I banged on the door and told her, "Listen miss, I don't know what is happening, but you have to come with me. Something bad is going on. You can't stay here. You've got to go. You've got to come with us."

She started crying and said that she was sorry. I told her not to be sorry, just to please come with me. She came with us and I took them down to the lobby.

I took them down using the freight elevator as the guest elevators had stopped. The New York City Police were downstairs. I guess they were escorting people who had just checked in. They were making sure that everything – and everyone - was safe. I immediately gave Leigh to the cops, and they escorted all three women out the side entrance to the downstairs, which lead to the bar and grill on the adjacent side of the lobby hotel.

After that, I never saw them again.

My Escape

Once I got out of the building, the towers came down. I didn't realize in the moment that I didn't have that much time to evacuate the area. I could have stayed there, perhaps another 5 to 10 minutes. If I had, I wouldn't be telling this story. The whole world just shook, and that's when I took off running. Big blue clouds of smoke overcame us like locusts. All I could utter was, "Oh my God."

When the first Tower came down, I actually thought I was dead because it was as if a white cloud had surrounded me. I didn't hear anything, and then a single beam of light pierced through that cloud and parted it like Jesus had done with the Red Sea. I could hear people all around me screaming, "Help, help, help, help, help!" That's when I knew that I was not dead.

My first thought was, "Wow, at least I made it to the right place."

I don't know how far I got, but I know I tripped. I thought I was as good as dead; I really did. I got far enough away from the scene to avoid being hit by any debris. I made it to the harbor where the boats were headed to New Jersey. At the end of the day, I was extremely lucky to have survived.

What happened to the woman in the wheelchair?

I always wondered what happened to Leigh. I thought about her frequently. Eight years later, I still wondered and did not know what happened to Leigh or her mother. I would think about them every anniversary of 9/11, wondering if they were alive or dead. I hoped they were fine.

I don't remember the day exactly or what year it was. I think it was in 2009 when I got a call from a friend of mine. He told me to turn the TV to the History Channel because they were showing a documentary on the hotel. He told me he thought the show was talking about Greg and me. I immediately turned on the History Channel, and sure enough I fell off the chair. I was so happy, I started to cry and laugh at the same time. I had such mixed emotions. I found out that Leigh and Faye were alive and doing well. They didn't know who I was, but I remembered Faye's face and I remembered the lady in the wheelchair. I always referred to Leigh as "the lady in the wheelchair" because at the time I didn't know what her name was.

The reunion

I called Ponce and told him to turn on the TV so he could see too. Ponce sent an email or some kind of correspondence to the TV station. The lady at the station told him that she couldn't release their contact information because it was confidential. However, she said she could give Leigh and Faye Ponce's contact information, and the two women could send him an email if they so desired. A couple days later, they reached out to Ponce. Ponce talked to them directly and told them who he was. That's when the whole surprise about who escaped together was revealed.

Chicago

We planned a reunion with about 8 years of history. They wanted to meet us in person.

The news picked up the story and they followed us from the time that we left New York to the time we arrived in Chicago.

We met Leigh and Faye in Chicago and the rest is history.

We were in Chicago for a joyous meeting with a lot of tears and laughter. We didn't know what had happened to each other. They were so grateful for our help that day and were so happy to see us. To this day, Faye and I are still in contact.

The passing of Leigh

It's unfortunate that Leigh, the daughter of Faye, passed away from multiple sclerosis. Still, I feel blessed to have been able to see her before she left us. She will be with me every day of my life until I am not here. I still keep in touch with Faye. Faye is like my Mom. She is the mother that I have in Chicago.

Reflections on surviving 9/11

I don't know why I am here - I really don't. I guess this experience may be the reason for me being here, yet I still don't really understand it. But I do know that Faye and Leigh will always be part of my family, no matter what.

I just want the world to know this: I was able to give them more years of their life, especially Leigh, because her life on this earth was spared on account of me. Furthermore, I will always have Faye as my "second mom" in Chicago. I keep in touch with her so she's never alone.

Sometimes our calling is way beyond us, and that's what happened to me. I happened to be at the right place. I don't know what made me think about Leigh and Faye. But I thought about them. Meeting them just popped into my head and I had to go and check to make sure that they were ok.

I'm not going to make a big deal about any hero stuff. It's a human thing. It was human nature for me to rescue those women. They started telling me I was a hero, but I didn't want to hear that. I was just a human being helping other human beings. We all live as one.

Faye took it a little further and so did Leigh, because she said, "If it wasn't for you, Greg, I wouldn't be here today." That hit me hard in my heart, and I really broke down crying. I couldn't take it anymore. Leigh said that even the firefighters told her that I had saved her life.

I'm so glad that I was able to reunite with Faye and Leigh. I miss Leigh, and I know that she was a tough woman and fought a good fight. I try not to bring her up because I don't want to make Faye upset, but every time she talks to me she starts crying. I don't want to be on the phone with her too long. I just check to see that she is fine.

I still think about the people who went to work that day and never came back – mothers, fathers, sisters, and brothers - and the fact that they did nothing to deserve their fate. What bothers me the most is that those people at the top of the towers had only two horrific choices: to jump or to burn to death.

And I ask God, "Can you imagine what was going through their minds?"

What a decision they had to make. It must have been so, so hard. I know that they are in a better place now. I hope that they didn't suffer. I hope it was quick and they are with God.

Meanwhile, I try to stay strong. It is important to live our lives to the fullest because we don't know how long we have in this world. Nobody ever expected to go to work that day and not come home. I live for them every day by telling this story to anyone who will listen.

No matter the day, may it be 14 or 15 years from now, the events of 9/11 will always feel as if they just happened yesterday. That's my story.

It's bittersweet, and it's something that I will always remember. I now have a 9/11 family because we all come from the same event, which will be engraved on our hearts for eternity.

Thank you for listening.

Greg (on right) with Ponce (left) and Leigh (Center) in Chicago (2009).

Faye, Greg and Leigh reunite in Chicago in 2009.

ILHAN K. GECKIL

A Turkey native is plagued with nightmares

Ilhan Geckil was traveling to NYC to attend the economics conference. He was filled with excitement over attending his first economics networking event. Ilhan was able to escape the ensuing disaster on September 11th, but what he saw at the World Trade Center haunts him for life. As a native of Turkey, he was reminded of the tragedy of his home country.

"I HEARD THE SOUND, AND I SAW THE CHANDELIERS SHAKING. WE LEFT THE BALLROOM IN PANIC."

In the morning (5am)

IT WAS 5AM on September 11. I was heading to the Marriott Hotel at the World Trade Center. It was the last day of the annual conference of the National Association of Business Economics. I had a flight back to Detroit later that afternoon. It was my first time attending the conference as an economist and I was very excited. I met many high profile business people and executives from all over the country, including the chief economists and vice presidents of many big companies.

It had been less than a year since I joined a consulting company in Michigan. This was the first big networking event for me. It felt good to be part of such an elite group. I earned my master's degree in economics from Michigan State University, and I was able to find a good job just after graduation.

As a native of Turkey, I came to the US for my education and to gain some work experience. I got a good undergraduate education at Koç University in Istanbul and studied graduate level economics at Michigan State University.

It was not my first visit to New York City, however this time I felt more privileged. I had a sense of being part of financial and economic circles.

The morning of September 11th, I headed to the WTC for the morning session of the last day of the NABE conference at 5am. I had not slept all night.

After graduating from Michigan State, it took some time for me to pay off my student loans and build my credit history. Since hotels in Manhattan were expensive, I could only afford to pay for three nights at the hotel. I was planning to spend the last night out with my college friends from Koç University and catch a couple hours of sleep in the hotel lobby before heading to the conference. I would attend the morning session of the conference and then head to the airport with my boss in the late afternoon.

My boss, Patrick, and I had already made plans. I was going to attend the morning breakfast and conference session, and meet up with him at the hotel lobby by 1 pm, have lunch together, and then take a cab to the airport.

It was September 11, 5 am in the morning, I had my small carry-on luggage and a brief case, and was heading to the Hotel at the World Trade Center. I spent all night out, around 2am that morning, I found a deli a couple blocks away from the hotel. I spent the following three hours at the deli eating, drinking coffee, and reading papers. After I left the deli, I went directly to the hotel with my carry-on luggage and brief case in tow.

At the hotel lobby

When I arrived, I found a remote corner with a sofa and put my belongings down. I was so tired I fell asleep right away. When I woke up it was 7:30

am. I heard the noises of people starting their day, arriving to the hotel for the conference. Since I had had two hours of deep sleep, I felt refreshed and ready for my last day in NYC. I was planning to leave my carry-on in storage at the hotel, however I decided to hide it behind the sofa and grab it after breakfast on my way out. I went to a restroom, washed my face, brushed my teeth and changed my clothes. I put my favorite canary yellow and navy tie on, making myself ready for the long day.

When I joined the conference crowd, it was almost 8 am. The previous day I had met some economists who had come all the way from Japan for the conference. I saw them and we exchanged pleasantries. They asked me if I had ever been to the observatory on the top floor of the World Trade Center. I said that I had not. They told me they were planning to go there after the breakfast meeting and that I was welcome to join them. I agreed to their offer. I had been here for four days and still had not gone all the way up to the top of the World Trade Center. I thought that was something I should do.

The shaking of the chandeliers

The speaker of the morning session was the chief economist, or strategy director of Morgan Stanley, and the title of his speech was "the Collapse of Wall Street!" After entering the breakfast ballroom, I sat at a table at the middle of the room with some economists from Michigan. It was a very nice room with chandeliers. I was trying to listen to the speaker while having my breakfast, however because I had only gotten of few hours of sleep the previous night, I was not able to concentrate. About 20 minutes into his speech, I heard that sound.

At around 8:45 am I heard that sound, and I saw the chandeliers shaking. I remember that moment as if it was yesterday - everybody was frozen for a second, and then alert in panic. I thought it was an earthquake or something.

As a Turk, I am familiar with such shaky situations. I remember the day I was leaving Istanbul in 1999. It was August 20, three days after the catastrophic earthquake that had killed tens of thousands of people.

I was familiar with earthquakes, but that sound? It was unlike anything I had ever heard before. We left the ballroom in a frightened but orderly fashion. We went to the hotel lobby. I looked outside and saw that a few cars had crashed and a man was lying on the street.

The lost luggage

When we were leaving the ballroom to get to the lobby, an attendee said that the incident might have been the result of a bomb. After seeing the scene outside, I thought the same. I was not in a panic; I was just trying to understand what happened.

And then I remembered my carry-on hiding behind the sofa. I went to pick that up, but it was not there. I ran to the receptionist desk at the lobby; they were in complete shock. Still, I needed to ask them where my luggage was. They directed me to the doorman desk. When I was heading to the desk, the hotel security and receptionist asked everybody to leave the hotel and run across the street. I needed to get my luggage. A doorman said they found my luggage behind the sofa and thought it was suspicious, so they took it to the storage area. I then began to get nervous, because if a bomb had in fact gone off, I thought they might question me due to my "suspicious" luggage. I could do nothing but leave the building.

With that concern in mind, I headed to the outside door of the hotel. A security guard was shouting, "Run across the street and do not look up!" I would not have looked up when I was running across the street, however since I was told not to do so, I naturally looked up. And what I saw was smoke.

About 5 minutes before 9 am I was across the street, among many curious and terrified people, and I looked up to the World Trade Center, wondering what happened. Some people were saying that a plane had hit the building. After staying there for about five minutes, I saw a plane approaching the World Trade Center. It hit the building before my eyes.

Out of pure fear and instinct, I ran to the side of the Hudson River. I could not believe what I saw. It looked like a scene from Hollywood movies. I felt that I was losing my sense of reality.

All of a sudden, I remembered a discussion I had had with some friends of mine in East Lansing, who were Ph.D. students in mechanical engineering and mathematics. Figen and Bulent had been telling me and some other friends of ours about the danger of automated defense systems, airplanes, missiles, etc. by the US government. If an error occurred, then the damage would be catastrophic, almost impossible to stop. I was scared even more by such a possibility and got closer to the river. If more planes started hitting the buildings or anywhere in Manhattan, I could jump into the water.

With such thoughts running through my mind and chain smoking having failed to calm my nerves, I eyed the top floors of the World Trade Center.

The most horrible scene

And then I saw the most horrible thing of my life, which would become part of my nightmares during the following years: people, desperate people jumping from the buildings. It was heartbreaking; I could not bear to watch any more. I started running north.

Countless police cars, fire trucks and other emergency vehicles were heading to the World Trade Center. I was running away from the WTC with many others.

After running five to six blocks, I turned right into the city streets and saw three people, two guys and a girl, getting into a cab. I shouted at them and they stopped. I asked them if I could share their cab. They told me they were heading to Midtown, and I said that that was fine. because I had a flight later that afternoon. After dropping them off, I would go to JFK. The cab driver told me that reports were saying all flights would be cancelled. I got into the cab anyway, and I told the cab driver Midtown would be fine. I didn't know NYC very well, so when the cab stopped, I had nothing to do but take off in the middle of Midtown along with my fellow riders.

Worried about my boss

My cell phone did not have reception, so I could not call anybody. I was worried about Patrick. *Was he able to leave the hotel in time. Was he ok?* I remembered his three young kids and felt terrible at the thought of something bad happening to him. I thought about my parents in Turkey. They might be very worried about me. Luckily, I did not tell them I was going to NYC. They thought I was in Michigan.

With all these thoughts and worries, I was walking around without any purpose. I saw a pub. In the moment, I thought that the best thing to do was to go there, watch the news and have something to drink. When I arrived at the pub, it was 10 minutes before 11 am.

A few drinks to settle my nerves

I asked the barman for a scotch, but he said they did not serve alcohol until 11 am. I told him I was in the WTC when the first plane hit the tower, and I could really use a drink. He gave me a shot. It was good. When I watched the news on CNN, I understood we were under an attack by terrorists and realized how great the tragedy was, and how lucky I had been to escape to safety.

After the third or fourth scotch, I used a public phone in the bar. I first called my girlfriend at the time. I told her that I was ok, and asked her stop crying and not worry. I called our office in East Lansing next, and I learned that my boss left the hotel in time and that he was ok as well. I was relieved by the news. Our office assistant told me that Patrick was going to meet me at the NYC building of Allianz. Apparently, one of his friends was a vice president at that company. He was going to wait for us in his office and then take us to his home in Rye.

I left the bar. The barman told me the drinks were on him.

Calling my mom to tell her I was alive.

When I arrived at Patrick's friend Paul's office, it was almost 2 pm. His office was on the 40-something floor of Allianz. I dreaded going up to a high floor in another high-rise. Paul welcomed me very warmly. Patrick was not there yet. He set me up in an office with a phone. I started calling my parents and friends. When I told my mother I was In NYC and I was ok, she started crying.

I did not need to tell her everything, so I chose not to tell her I was actually at the World Trade Center when the terrorist attacks happened.

After half an hour, Patrick arrived. We hugged; it was really good to see him. We left Manhattan to to stay with Paul for the following two days.

Since all flights were cancelled, Patrick and I rented a car two days after our stay at the house.

It was September 13th , and I was leaving New York City with one thought in my mind: there was a reason I was in NYC, at the WTC, and experienced such tragedy.

I had tears in my eyes on the road remembering those who chose to jump from the building in desperation. I knew back then, and I know now, that I will never forget the attacks on 9/11.

DIANA I. GREGG

An economic journalist from Washington DC escapes

Diana Greg was in Room 617 inside the hotel in the World Trade Center when the first plane hit. She was in New York City to cover the business economics conference for her company. Some of her belongings were sent back to her by NYPD three years later.

"I DIDN'T LOOK BACK BECAUSE I UNDERSTOOD WHAT THE SOUND MEANT – THAT EVERYONE INSIDE: THE FIRE FIGHTERS, THE PEOPLE TRAPPED, WERE DEAD."

I'M AN ECONOMIC journalist, now retired, and I was at the Marriott WTC covering the annual meeting of the National Association for Business Economics for my company, and had been there since Sunday afternoon. When the first jet hit, I was in my room on the sixth floor and went to the window which faced West Street. What I saw was so disturbing – chunks of cement raining down on the street and cars swerving to avoid being hit – that I left immediately, taking only my purse and a small reporter's notebook; no laptop or bag.

I came out of the stairwell at the mezzanine floor and coming down the big staircase I heard for the first time that a plane had hit the tower. I exited the Marriott through the side entrance where the Tall Ships restaurant was after telling two Marriott employees that there was a woman on my floor, directly across from my room, who was on a motorized scooter and would need help getting out. Then I crossed West Street and went into a building that had public phones in the lobby; hard to believe today but back then I did not own a cell phone.

I called my husband, Tom, who had not yet left for work; I told him to let my office know I had gotten out – we still thought it was some freak accident involving a small airplane—and to also contact our daughter, a college student doing a semester abroad in Australia. According to my credit card, the call was at 9; I was back out on the street just right before the United Airline jet slammed into the South Tower.

One minute I was talking to a stranger on the street and the next I was screaming and running toward the Hudson. I remember thinking that it was an attack and yet could not figure out who or why. I retained that image of the nose of the jet, which clearly meant it was a commercial jet, not a military plane or a missile, and so there had to be people inside.

Not long after that, the horrific sight of the exploding jet was replaced by the equally horrific sight of men jumping from the North Tower. I would see a piece of debris float down and the next time I looked up it would be a man.

So I kept moving along the esplanade, hugging the river, talking to strangers – one man told me about two hijacked planes from Logan – and moving south, not because I knew where I was going but because I wanted to stay by the water in case there was another attack. I passed people who looked dazed and people who were pushing strollers or had dogs in tow. I passed a young woman who was sobbing and thought I should comfort her but could not do anything.

At one point I went into a Gristedes because someone told me they had coffee there and my nerves were shot. When I came back out on the street, the flames from the towers were a brighter orange, the smoke more black, and I could still see someone jump but was now too far to tell if it was a man or a woman.

When the South Tower fell, I must have been close to Battery Park;

there was a sound like a gigantic wave and we all pushed forward, not running in a panic but moving quickly. I didn't look back because I understood what the sound meant – that everyone inside: the fire fighters, the people trapped, were dead.

The ashes rained down, the sky got very dark. There was a young woman next to me who was carrying a toddler and she pulled the baby's shirt over his head. I looked at a man whose eyes were bloodshot and realized I must look the same.

A policeman told us to move ahead toward a clearing, away from any building, which is how I came to be standing by an old fort, Castle Clinton, when the North Tower fell. I was standing around with two men in their 20s and two women and we sought shelter in the deep windows of the fort and stayed there until the second wave of ashes settled.

I discovered the two young guys were not New Yorkers but from Fayetteville, Arkansas, and had been at the same NABE conference at the Marriott that I had been covering. So now we had to figure out how we were going to get out of Manhattan and home. They were very nice, and now I was not alone in the middle of this crisis.

When we saw a ferry coming, one of them suggested we get on. I had misgivings about being in the middle of the river when who knew what else was out there but then Tyler took my hand and I managed to get over my fear. I can't describe how awful the sight of the skyline was from the deck of the ferry; the towers were gone and dark gray smoke billowed from the ruins, filling the sky. I wanted to weep.

In Jersey City, they had organized volunteers with damp towels and bottled water who directed us to buses that would take us to Newark Penn Station. At this point I was looking around for anyone who might be a journalist to get more news of Washington. I already knew about the attack on the Pentagon but there were other stories, of a car bomb outside the State Department and another at the Supreme Court. People were generous with their cell phones but I could not get through to DC; it would be close to four o'clock before I finally talked to my family.

In Newark, I got on a train to Trenton. Trenton looked green and bucolic, a world away from the chaos and ashes of New York. There was a man on the train who worked on the 31st floor of the North Tower. He described walking down the stairs, knowing this was no accident, and seeing the firemen walking up while everyone else was hurrying down. He told me that if I had been looking at the North Tower from the side street where the first jet went in, I would have realized this was no small commuter plane.

In Trenton, I found out Union Station was open and I was able to take the Metroliner home. I was reunited with my husband and talked to my daughter on the phone. Luckily, she had not been checking her email, and so did not know where I had been staying in New York.

Three years after 9/11, I was reunited with my luggage, the small carry-on bag I had left on the bed. The NYPD contacted me in June 2004; Jerry, a property specialist with the World Trade Center Project, told me he had just one item to go on, a ground transportation receipt, issued to a "Ms. Gregg" by Delta at LaGuardia. It took months of research but it eventually led to the NABE website and to me.

"They're dirty," Jerry said when I asked about the condition of my clothes. When the bag arrived, I was amazed everything had not been pulverized; the jeans were ripped, the shoes bent, but a favorite plaid blouse was perfectly wearable.

Most meaningful to me were the Frommer's *Walking Tours New York* and my reporter's notebook. The guide book belonged to my husband, who passed away in late 2003. It was also a reminder of my own mortality. On the margins of one page I had checked the suggestion to go up to the 107th floor observation deck, and had intended to do that before flying home Tuesday afternoon.

As it turned out, I went up to the 107th floor observation deck of the North Tower on Monday night Sept. 10, first alone after dinner at the Marriott and then a second time with my friend Joan, who was also at the conference. We were awed by the view which seemed to stretch into infinity. To this day I wonder whether if I had not gone up Monday night, I might have been doing just that at 8:30 on Tuesday morning.

September 11 was a transformative experience, because it was so painful to be present where so many died. Today, with the recent horrors of Paris and San Bernardino, we are again more aware of terrorism. But I don't think that is a reason to give up on our way of life, and give in to fear and the forces of intolerance.

MATTHEW HARTTREE

*A North Carolinian, forever indebted
to the hero that saved him*

---

*Matthew Harttree is a lead systems engineer with a communications
software company. Since 9/11, he has focused his career on building
critical emergency communications systems. His research focuses on
large-scale real-time data correlation used by crisis management
personnel. On 9/11, he was caught in the collapse and is now a
tireless advocate of increased access to alternative recovery therapies
such as VRIT/VRET for individuals suffering from post-traumatic
stress. He has never forgotten the multiple sacrifices that were
made to save his life that Tuesday morning.*

"THE PRESSURE WAS SO INTENSE. IT WAS LIKE I WAS
GETTING SQUEEZED FROM ALL SIDES. I STILL HAVE
LUNG PROBLEMS PROBABLY TO THIS DAY. YOU ARE
BREATHING IN JUNK AND IT HURTS AND YOU'RE
COUGHING UP BLOOD."

NEW YORK IS not a cheap place to rent a hotel room of any measure. I'm a southern guy and I was honestly astounded by the rates. I found out that the bank that I was working for, along with a lot of other companies involved with this large project, were staying at the Marriott World Trade Center. We ended up getting a long-term rate for at the Marriott World Trade Center. That Monday, I arrived in New York. I had gotten in Monday a little late and was delayed getting in - I had missed one flight and taken a later one. So when I got to work, I stayed late.

On September 11, I had to do a presentation that Tuesday afternoon. Like most IT projects, you work in phases. I had to prepare for the meeting, so I really didn't need to be at the customer site bright and early. I was pleased that I could sleep in a little bit and have some leisure time to possibly work out. The hotel had a nice fitness center on the floor above me, so the game plan was to sleep in a little bit, wake up and then start my day.

What I do remember is that the day started late. I was on the 21st floor of the hotel in Room 2130, which faced out over the West Side Highway towards the Hudson River. If I opened my curtains, I could see that I was above the World Financial Center, the place with the green tops. When I woke up that morning around 8:15 am, I neglected to open the shades and hopped in the shower. Towards the end of my shower, I heard a loud noise. I thought at first something simply was wrong with the water in the hotel.

Being on the 21st floor maybe something had gone wrong, but the sounds were quite echo-y and disturbing. I later surmised that this was likely when the first airplane hit the hotel. Little did I know at the time it was more than just creaky pipes.no into the trade center and later found out that you know didn't know, but there was a whole huge thud above me.

From what I understand, they found parts of the plane, such as the engine, ravaging the roof of the Marriott. A piece of it landed in the pool in the workout center on the 22nd floor.

It almost blows my mind that if 9/11 had happened today, people would know instantly what was going on via social media. Yet only 15 short years ago, nobody really had a clue as the events unfolded.

I turn on the TV and was getting bad pictures on the TV for some reason. I was throwing on some clothes. I opened the curtains and I looked out. If you craned your neck and stood right up against the curtain, looking down, I see a bunch of fire trunks coming down the west side highway. There's a whole bunch of like papers and crud flying by the window like insulation or something. Then the first real major idea that something had gone wrong for me was a larger chunk of something went flying down the window and I was like "that's not good."

You have something that is out of the ordinary and then, I made a phone call. I was married at the time and made a phone to my wife and was like "hey something's up." You know, again information didn't travel that fast. I don't think there was really anything that quickly broken on the news. I think the first thing that I saw on the news as I was fiddling with the channels, still getting dressed, was that a small plane had hit the World Trade Center. I remember hearing stories from a relative or something had happened kind of like that to the Empire state building and so at the time I didn't realize what extreme calamity was occurring.

"It's a horrible loss for the people on the plane," I thought. But I could have never imagined the extent of the damage and destruction that would occur.

Around that time, it was getting closer to 9 o'clock. I was fully dressed. There was a knock on the door. It was a hotel porter, who in hindsight saved many people's lives, including my own. He was just running around through the hall, knocking on people's doors. There was a detective or somebody that was with him and he knocked on my door, knocked on it twice. Quick tap on the door and I opened the door as he was walking away, thinking I was already leaving. That's when I really heard the fire alarm go off in the hotel. It sounded warbled and defective – that's the best way that I can describe it. There were other folks that told me they didn't hear it go off initially. I assumed that the impact of the plane hitting the hotel had affected the fire alarm's vibrancy, because I didn't hear it ringing in my room.

The hotel porter looked at me and I looked at him.

He told me, "You need to get out of here. You are not supposed to be here."

I didn't know what he meant, but apparently they had started

evacuating the hotel. I stupidly grabbed a roller backpack with me thinking, "Hey it's going to be fine day." I headed out the door and heard something going on, but nothing was really connecting in my mind. I was just
thinking that everything was fine. I went to press the button on the elevator and he stopped me from doing it.

"You know you can't do that," he said, and pointed me to the stairs.

I walked all the way down the corridor to the other side where he had
directed me - which would have been near the fire exit at the corner of
West and Liberty Streets. I proceeded to make my way down the stairs,
lugging this backpack full of project paperwork. I was headed down the
stairs at a pretty decent pace, so the papers started falling out of the bag
and creating a mess. 21-20-19-18 seconds. The clock was ticking and little
did I know how precious those seconds were.

I got down to probably around 11, 12 or 13 seconds and I'm still kind
of oblivious to everything that is going on. I'm one of the last ones out
of the building. The stairs seemed to go on forever, and meanwhile I was
struggling with my bag. So I'm down to about 13-12-11 seconds by time
I've hit the 11th floor, at which point I had started to get a really good
rhythm going. I was carrying my bag in one hand and bracing myself
against the inside of stairwell as I turned around every corner.

All I could think was, "I've just got to get out of here."

I felt annoyance creeping in at how long it was taking me to get out of
the building, but annoyance quickly turned to fear. There was this tremendous echo-y sort of thud as I flew around the corner, and I simultaneously
got my leg jammed in a piece of the stair rail. It's the one thing I distinctly
remember, while the rest is a blur. I don't know if airborne is the right
word, but I was completely knocked off balance - having the bag in my
other hand didn't help either. When I finally settled on the ground, I was
hurting and struggling to get my leg out of there. My knee was all messed
up from the incident and I was getting scared. The building began to violently shake, and that's when I knew that something was up.

Then I was at a slower pace, 11-10-9 going down the flight of stairs.
I was limping and my knee still hurt, not to mention my problems were
exacerbated by the bag I had with me. You know any intelligent person

would have just ditched the bag, but I was still thinking that I was going to my meeting that day.

I got down to the third floor and spotted what I assumed was an emergency exit. It was one of those doors with a huge glowing sign that said if you open it, an alarm would sound. I was still limping when I heard a fire alarm go off. Following that cue, I guessed that this situation qualified as an emergency.

✥

I'm very much a law and order guy type, so I stupidly sat for a second outside of the door, still kind of limping in pain and struggling with a sore knee. I remember looking at the door for a second wondering whether I should open it, but I finally pushed it open. I was thinking lights and sirens were going to go off, but surprisingly there was only a weak, low battery warble, which I thought was kind of a little ironic given the circumstances. I opened the door and it was World War III outside. It wasn't good.

There was a firefighter out on the street and a sheet half covering the remains of a body. When I opened the door and saw him, he looked at me and then looked up. It seemed to be the running theme of the day for people to be surprised to see me.

The firefighter yelled to me, "Do not let that door close," and I instantly jumped into action.

I immediately grabbed the door, but it already kind of bent because something had happened to it, so it was tough to open. I don't know if something had hit it, I just remember it being tough to work. He was yelling at me to get back inside and I was yelling at him to get me out of there.

He screamed, "It's not f***ing safe, get the f**k back inside!"

The interaction quickly degenerated into a New York street conversation involving New York street adjectives - it's the best way I can describe it. I was starting to really panic, but that man - I'll never really know who he was - jolted me into thinking that something was really wrong. By dealing with me in his direct, authoritative manner, he made me realize that I needed to start paying attention and stop moaning and groaning about trivial complaints – like being late or having to walk down the stairs.

As I was sitting outside the hotel, I noticed a hole in the concrete.

Something metal had fallen while we were talking and now it was sticking out of the ground.

I don't remember what it was or how it got there, but I remember looking at it and thinking, "That's kind of odd that that is just sticking out of the concrete. That's definitely not a good sign."

There was also a body there and a sea of fire trucks and EMS vehicles.

I heeded the firefighter's advice and headed back inside. The hotel had a conference area on the second and third floor in the business center and a catering area in the back in the hotel kitchen. I started making my way back, even though I didn't really know the layout of the hotel. That experience taught me an important lesson I still value to this day. If I check into a hotel, I will spend 15 minutes and figure out where I am. Because looking back at 9/11, my ignorance nearly got me killed. It's a lesson that I have passed onto my son and I'm very grateful that he kind of picks up on it and does it on his own. Spending a couple of minutes locating the emergency exits in a facility and listening for announcements can make all the difference in an emergency situation..

I made my way back up one flight of stair and spotted another set down a hallway. I bumped into a gentlemen who was apparently running late as well. However, he seemed to handle himself with relative ease and was quite calming, as I was currently amped and nervous.

In his reassuring way he said, "We are going to get out of here. Let's figure out what's going on."

I was still carrying the freaking laptop roller bag - and laptops back in 2001 weren't light things like the iPads of today - so naturally I was tired and stressed as we headed down the hallway.

I took a turn and ended up going through a service entrance and coming out into the hallway where the conference rooms were. We made our way into a large semicircular staircase, to the left of the main entrance, because the elevators had all been knocked out. I just remember looking down from the top of the stairs toward the lobby and seeing it filled with firefighters and law enforcement. What I learned later was that they had been moving people across the street in groups through the Tall Ships Bar, and then they would ride them into the financial center, check everybody in and then get them out of the area.

All this was happening around 9:30 am. It was starting to get pretty dicey outside. As I was walking down the stairs and still trying to figure out if/how I was going to get out, I encountered a nicely dressed man - possibly hotel security or police - who said that I needed to go check in with a different gentleman. The nicely dressed man was calm and I can't speak highly enough of him.

It turned out he wasn't a police officer but was the assistant manager of the hotel. He just was promoted to assistant manager direct He directed me to a man named Joe stationed in the middle of the lobby. As I was standing there with my bag, Joe asked if he could help me. I pulled out the key card to my room and he looked kind of surprised. He must have wondered what I was still doing there in the hotel, because most of the guests had already been evacuated.

"I'll stay out of your way," I said.

I was going to head back upstairs to use the business center to make a few phone calls, as my cell phone wasn't working at the time. It was all jammed up because everybody apparently in Lower Manhattan was trying to make phone calls at the same time.

"No you're not," Joe said. "You are going to walk over towards the visitors in the payphone area."

He directed me to the congregating area for guests and visitors, which was at the corner of West and Liberty Streets. We were trying to find a way to get out to the area and I remember hearing some thuds turned out later that you know it wasn't a good thing happening on the hotel's you know skylight roof. Someone told me not to look up and I'm pretty grateful that I didn't. I'm sure that image would have haunted me forever. I know someone that did and they are still having problems with it to this day

I went over to sit by the hotel and start making some phone calls on the calling card. It was around 9:50 am and there were a bunch of other folks in the hotel. I wandered over to the front desk to try and make another phone call because the pay phones were kind of jammed up. The woman at the desk was extremely helpful and polite. I hope to be able to reach out and say thank you to her now because she had a composure above and beyond what you would expect of any employee. Her name was Amy and she was fantastic. I remember seeing her name badge so if you ever on a side note outside of the interview if you ever find out where she's at these days I would love to drop her a 15 year over note and say thank you because I was never able to get in touch with her and she was working the front desk right there

Amy was fantastic. Joe was there and I mean for the couple remaining people in the corner, I don't know if I think that there were a couple contract service workers or like folks that the hotel had contacted to work on something that day or something along those lines and so there were just folks kind of mingling about using the phones and I was trying to stay out of the way and then I realized that a couple firefighters had come in and um and were coming in to use the payphones so I kind of wanted to make sure and actually I remember making a couple calls for him because one guy didn't have all the quarters and nickels he needed

He made a call on my calling card and simply told the voice on the other end of the line, "Hey, I'm going to be late."

I remember watching them gather their gear and seeing on their tags that they were from Ladder 118 - apparently they had driven all the way in from Brooklyn as a back up and now they were at the front entrance to the World Trade Center itself. This is one detail that will always stick out in my mind, as it reminds me of the vast extent of loss that was experienced that day.

The central lobby was now quite crowded, so they started using the hotel entrance as a way to get to the World Trade Center since everything was interconnected (you could walk in through the hotel lobby, hang a left, walk down the short corridor and you were right in the World Trade Center). So they were streaming in as I was on the phone. A few came in and started heading up the stairs to check some other areas of the hotel for damage. I turned my back and picked up the phone again. For whatever reason, I was able to get my calling card to work, so when I called my dad, the line connected.

When I got ahold of him, he was watching the news at a place he was working at the time. They had a TV, and he started telling me what was going on. I think I got a little emotional and began cursing up a storm. It was close to 10 am.

The best way I can describe what happened next is that it sounded like

I was directly under a freight train. The oddest thing was that the pressure so was intense. It was like I was getting squeezed from all sides. I was on the phone with my dad and then the whole place in a split second went black. Some people talked about the events happening in slow motion, and I guess in hindsight it probably seemed as if they did. It was just so odd - we heard this huge sound and then the whole place went black.

Next, I was airborne. I got picked up as the South Tower was crushing the hotel - the force and the pressure of it all of that air had to go somewhere, all of that force had to go somewhere. It just knocked the living crud out of me and next thing you know. All I've got in my hands I'm getting beamed in the head, hit in the head with stuff and my bag is no longer with me. stupid freaking computer bag. I think I had a piece of the phone in my hand or something like that and then I'm on the floor. I got gunk in my mouth, I got gunk in my eyes. I was able to find my glasses like they were kind of like crimpled, but I was able to see something out of them.

It was a horrific scene. And I couldn't breathe. There were some people around me that were no longer alive and some were on the hotel floor just trying to find a way out of there. We couldn't see anything.

There were some people that were moaning, but nobody was screaming really loud. I got blood on me from other folks. We must have been stuck in there for a little while, I don't know the exact amount of time. A wall collapsed on the side of the wall toward West Street, which there's a picture of that is out on the internet. The pressure became too much for the outside walls of the hotel and a portion of it fell open. That's when we could see the light coming in. My ears were ringing and I couldn't really hear anything. I rolled or walked or limped or whatever. My knee was killing me I had gotten pelted in the back. I was bleeding out of my back it was cuts, scraps that kind of stuff. My head had gotten knocked pretty. I went out that little exit - that little place where the wall had collapsed. We went outside the west side. I think we figured out sometime it was 10:15. I went outside. My memory around this gets pretty fuzzy but what I do we remember is I went outside. I got sick or whatever trying to breath, but the other thing I do remember is when I was able to clear my lungs out and take that first breath of air. I took in once I was able to clear my lungs out is something that I'll never forget.

I was breathing in ash. I still have lung problems probably to this day. You know you are breathing in junk and it hurts and you're coughing up blood. Then to finally to get outside - even as bad as the air was out there – and to be able to breathe was a miracle.

Across the street, I think I blacked out. It's like little snapshots after that, I recall that someone – likely a serviceman - carried me across the street, which was not a small feat as the street was a double lane highway in either direction. Once I was placed on the other side of the road, my ears kind of opened up. That's when I really started hearing just a mess of people screaming and yelling in sheer terror.

I ducked – or rather limped - into a small restaurant that was nearby. As I was trying to get oriented to my surroundings, all I could hear was these alarms. The shrill noise of them stuck with me for years. Someone explained to me that if you are walking around as you move, it prevents an alarm from going off. But if you're standing still or down on the ground as you pass these alarms, they go off. And on this day, I sadly remember that they would not stop ringing.

Inside the restaurant was an EMS personnel who gave me some oxygen. Right around that time, the second tower came down and it was just like here we go again. It was evident that where we were wasn't safe; although ironically everybody that was in there, (about five to 10 people) had ducked into that place for a few seconds to get their bearings. We were just looking at each other.

We were like, "We have got to get out of here."

People started screaming out that the second crash had occurred in the World Financial Center, across West Street from the World Trade Center.

I didn't know New York at the time. That is the other thing I learned from traveling - to take some time to get to know the city, get to know where you are. I have learned to become more aware of my situation because at any moment this knowledge could save your life. I merely had a tourist guidebook to New York City upon my arrival. It had a hole in it. I shoved it into my back pocket when I left the hotel room because I knew that I did not have anything until my meeting later, so I thought I might get in some sights beforehand. I still happened to have it in my back pocket while I was crawling around on the floor. I tried to take it out and it was in tatters. The only thing left visible on the pages was the Hudson River.

I was in Battery Park City, and somehow I managed to walk all the way to the railing near the river. I was about to jump in because simply put, I needed to get off that island.

This was just in time but then a New York City police boat was to my left, and a man on the boat shouted to me, "Don't jump, just come down here."

They put me on the boat and I passed out for a bit. I was then taken to a drop off point across the river, put in an ambulance and taken to the hospital, where I ended up staying for a while. A couple weeks later, I got a phone call from the hotel doorman. He and I have remained friends to this day. He let me know that Joe had directed me to the right place. If I had gone up to the business center of the hotel, I would have been dead. Joe, along with pretty much everybody from Ladder 118 and obviously everyone else, but the folks that were in the hotel, they died

Joe Keller saved my life and many of other people's lives that day.

After I recovered in the hospital, I went home. I took some time off and got a whole bunch of medical situations resolved.

⚛

It has been 15 years and I still do not like to talk too much about it. I just prefer to be the quiet guy, but I think that this survivors project is important. It's important that I tell the story for this book, as my account keeps the history of the events alive. That is why I talk about it. For me, the retelling of my story allows healing to happen – which I'm sure is the case for many other survivors as well. Still, the trauma resulting from these events is something I continually struggle with.

There were many amazing people that day - law enforcement, firefighters, first responders - that were thrust into really difficult situations. There were a lot of uncommon people doing uncommon things. Abdul, the assistant manager, was the breadwinner of his family. He was the person that was going after the American dream. His true character shined when someone simply said, "I need your help." He knew that hotel like the back of his hand. Abdul was, for a lot of people, the invisible face that a guest may or may not think about. But he knew just exactly how to handle the terrible situation with grace and finesse.

There was also Joe Keller. I mean, one of his children is the same age as mine - that always sticks with me. He was somebody who really excelled at customer service and lived to do his job well - or any job he was given for that matter. Many people that I have talked to acknowledge this about him.

I talked to Rose, his wife, after he died. She was an amazing woman, and he came from an amazing family. He was one of those people that when the chips were down, and he knew something was terribly wrong at the hotel, he still chose to stay and help others. He didn't have to be there – security and most everyone else had already left. He stayed at his own peril. For both Joe and Abdul, their decisions to stay cost them their lives. Still, Joe ultimately saved my life, knowing that the safest place for me was in the corner of the hotel. And that's where he sent everybody and made sure that everyone was there.

As for the men from Ladder 118, there's a picture of the aftermath of the destruction that reminds me of them – those brave souls who left Brooklyn around 9 am and were in the midst of the chaos by about 9:30 am. Many others would have looked at that mess in the skyline and said, "This is not something I want to be near," but hundreds of folks – including those from Ladder 118 - poured into the building and attempted to help in any way that they could. Ultimately, their selflessness cost them their lives.

The men from the NYPD tactile marine unit saw me, as well as countless others, at the right time, and they helped me breathe again. They worked some 30 hours straight; one of them even worked 40 hours because he was coming in from the holdover shift from the night before. The determination and altruism exhibited by these individuals is something that will always stick with me.

I'm very grateful to be here today, just as I'm sure everyone is who made it out of that hotel or was located in Lower Manhattan that day. I am always reminded how easily my experience could have gone the other way.

Therefore, I kiss my kids and say a nice prayer for those who do not have the opportunity to do the same.

CATHY PIWOWARCZYK HOFFMANN

A Missouri survivor befriends a diabetic in need

Cathy Hoffman was a university fundraiser from Missouri and was staying in Room 1116 of the Marriott hotel at the World Trade Center. It was her first trip to New York in seven years. She helped a diabetic woman and they clung onto each other during the day. Witnessing the attacks left a devastating impact on her. Cathy's life would never be the same after surviving these attacks.

"THE DUST WAS COVERING US AND I WAS HAVING A HARD TIME MOVING QUICKLY OR BREATHING."

ON SEPTEMBER 8, 2001, I flew to Newark, New Jersey to spend a few days with a friend before going to Manhattan for a week-long business trip. After spending the weekend in New Jersey, my friend drove me to my hotel at the World Trade Center.

My first impression of the hotel was that it was a gorgeous facility, especially as it was sandwiched between the two towers of the World Trade Center. On Monday, I had several appointments with my employer and dinner in the hotel restaurant. I knew the next day that I had a very important meeting at 10 am, so I spent the evening getting all of my resource material together. I made sure my alarm was set and a wakeup call was set as well.

The next morning on September 11, I was up early for my appointment. I knew I had time for breakfast, so I went to the downstairs café. I had a light breakfast and read my book. I went back to my room at 8 am and got in the shower. After showering and putting on my makeup, I started packing my portfolio with the day's materials. I looked outside and saw the bright sun and beautiful blue clouds and was sure it was going to be a great day. I knew that my morning meetings coupled with an afternoon spent shopping in little Italy with my friend from New Jersey were going to be grand. I phoned my friend to confirm our afternoon, and no sooner had I done so that I heard a loud *BOOM* and felt the entire hotel shake.

My first thought after the noise and shake was that a wrecking ball must have hit the building. I knew there was construction going on outside the building, so this was the most logical explanation I could think of. I looked out the window again, which faced West Highway, and saw a young blond woman looking up at our building with the most horrified look on her face I had ever seen. I looked down in front of the hotel and many cars and taxis were crashing into each other.

It was at that moment I realized something more serious than a wrecking ball had hit the World Trade Center.

My first thought was to call my mother in St. Louis. I figured she always had the news on in the morning so she would know what was happening. It never occurred to me to turn on my own television. Unfortunately, my mother, being retired, was still sleeping. She hurried to the kitchen and turned on the TV. She said they were showing a fire in one of the towers. I didn't smell any smoke, so told her I was sure things were fine. I called downstairs and asked her to hold on since I had called her on my cell phone.

I called downstairs and they said they didn't know what was going on either. I asked if we should evacuate, and they said that was probably a good idea. I conveyed this information to my mother and told her I was going to finish getting ready and would call her again as soon as I could.

I finished getting dressed for my meetings, packed all my information in my laptop case, brushed my teeth and prepared to leave the room. As I walked past the bathroom, I saw my medications and thought I had enough for the day so I would be alright. At that time, I had a serious disease called Reflex Sympathetic Dystrophy, which caused my legs to swell and lose mobility for long periods of time.

"Do you know what happened?"

As soon as I opened my hotel room door, two things were very odd. First, there was no one else in the hallway. It was silent. Second, a strange, strong smell hit me right away. I had no idea what the smell was.

I immediately went to the stairway in the center of the hall.

As I got in the stairwell, there were several other individuals coming down the stairs from floors above me. We exchanged pleasantries, and everyone began asking the same question, "Do you know what happened?"

No one knew anything, but we all agreed going down to the lobby was our best idea.

I was in the first group of people going down the steps when we reached the third or fourth floor. We noticed at that time there were very large cracks in the concrete walls. We were all concerned and discussed going back up a flight and down the other stairwell at the end of the hall. We agreed that this might be a good idea as we did not know what the cracks could mean.

So, we went to the other stairwell and descended to the lobby. As we got close to the lobby door, we were able to see outside. It looked like a bomb had gone off. There was dust and debris as far as the eye could see.

Some of the people began crying and getting very scared. As we opened the door to the lobby, we heard a great deal more crying and screaming. The lobby was very full. No one had any information, but we did see a few people leaving out the side door. This side door became our target to reach. Some people were pushing and shoving, but most were kind and moved as efficiently as possible.

At some point, we saw paramedics coming through the lobby. On the stretcher was a terribly burned woman who was visibly upset and scared. I believe seeing this woman scared many people, and the crying and screaming intensified. My goal was to get out of the hotel and find a taxi to get to my appointment at the other end of Manhattan. I had no inclination that anything was going to keep me from getting to my appointment.

While making our way from one end of the lobby to the other, there was a very large noise and again the building shook. Since the walls to the outside were glass, we were able to see a lot of debris and things raining down from above. The panic in the lobby grew even greater. Sometime during this ordeal, I began crying and didn't even realize it. There were a few tables in the lobby with napkins, so I took one to use, knowing I would give it back that evening.

As we got to the side door, I heard a policeman saying, "Cover your head and RUN."

This concerned me because I hadn't been to New York in seven years, so I had no idea where to go. I asked the people around me and they didn't know either. So when it was my turn at the door - they were letting us out the door in groups of two and three - I asked the policeman where to go. He pointed to another policeman on the other side of West Highway and said, "Cover your head and run to him."

I had my purse and laptop case with me, so was I unsure how to cover my head. I figured if I could get across the highway, I could find a taxi and get to my appointment. It took me a great deal of time to get to the other side of the highway since I couldn't run with my disease and what I was carrying, and I had to dodge a variety of obstacles in the street.

When I reached the policeman on the other side, he saw that I was in a great deal of pain and was having trouble walking. He asked me if I needed medical attention. After seeing the woman on the stretcher in the lobby and figuring there must be more like her, I told him that I could make it on my own (several years later, I realized if I had said yes and he put me in one of the ambulances by the hotel, I would likely have been crushed in the ambulance when the towers and hotel collapsed).

Once I was out of the hotel and across the highway, my immediate goal was to find a taxi and get to my appointment. I was simply following everyone on the sidewalk.

Looking down, I was shocked by everything on the ground - from purses and wallets to cameras and computers. I still didn't know what was going on and couldn't figure out why people would have dropped those things.

As I walked, I began looking for a store or building that might have a phone since all of our cell phones weren't working. I thought I saw a small store a block or two ahead, so my goal was to reach it. I needed to walk forward a bit and then turn right after about a block.

As I turned off of West Highway, it was the first time I looked backward and saw the fire and the gaping hole in one of the towers. I knew things were very serious now.

As I reached the store, there was a long line to use the phone. Looking ahead, I saw people converged around a car and thought that one of their phones might be working. There was a group of four or five men around the car and I asked them if they knew what was going on in the towers. They each looked at me as if I was crazy and said, "Don't you know, it's a terrorist attack."

I said there was no way it was a terrorist attack, and then they told me about the Pentagon and the other plane that went down in the field. I knew it was more crucial than ever to find a phone to call my mother to reassure her I was out of the hotel and was ok. I went into an office and told the people there about my situation, and they were kind enough to let me use their landline to call Missouri.

The call to my mother

I was very surprised to hear my mother's emotion when she heard my voice. I really hadn't realized the magnitude of the situation. After I was off the phone, I went back outside to the street and sat on the curb and prayed. It wasn't long after I sat down that I felt my feet shake and heard a rumble. Looking down the street to the towers I saw the first tower fall.

I went into shock and couldn't move.

Several people came toward me and helped me get up and back into the office where I had used the phone.

At this time, many other people came to the office, including mothers with babies and people with their dogs. All of them were covered in dust and having a hard time breathing. Many of us went to the faucets in the restrooms and the water fountains to get wet towels for all the people that needed them.

After some time, a gentleman asked if there was a doctor in the house. A man next to me said he was a doctor but he wasn't getting involved for fear someone would sue him. The same gentleman that had asked for a doctor then announced he was going to get a head count, and at that same moment another person yelled, "The second tower is going, run!"

Everyone followed the instructions and tried pushing out the door and running. Again, not knowing where I was, I was just following everyone running alongside the water (later I learned we were running through Battery Park). The dust was covering us and I was having a hard time moving quickly or breathing. Up ahead, quite a few people were stopping at what looked like a boat dock. The line was getting very long and I only saw one boat. I didn't think there would be any way I could get on that boat, so I just kept moving forward.

At some point, the wind picked up and shifted, allowing us to breathe a bit better. Most people were taking a seat on the concrete planters around the trees in Battery Park.

A diabetic in need

I hadn't been sitting there for more than five to ten minutes when a woman came up to me and said she had seen that I had a laptop bag, and was hoping I might have a candy bar or something sweet in it. She said she was evacuated from her apartment in Battery Park and had left with no shoes, purse nor medication. She said she was a diabetic, and since she didn't have her medication, she needed something sweet. I didn't have any candy but had a few cough drops with me. She said those would work. We sat and talked for a bit and she told me her name was Lori.

The boat ride that took us to New Jersey

A short time after that, a boat pulled up to the railing near where we were sitting. The captain said he would take women and children first, and the men nearby formed a line to help the women and children over the iron railing and into the boat. It was difficult for me since I had my purse and laptop, so the men took those from me and helped me into the boat.

Lori and I sat together on the boat and talked to each other and the people around us. It was one of those people who told us she worked for a car rental company. She said that all of their black sedans had been rented for the day. When I asked why that was, she said the people responsible for the 1993 bombing of the WTC were being sentenced that day. Once she told us that information, we all felt that the terrorist attacks made more sense.

The boat took us across the Hudson River and dropped us off onto land. I had to ask Lori where we were because I had no clue. She said that we were in New Jersey. Close by was a type of hotel/motel. I was aware of the chain of command and knew that they had a type of commissary. I knew that if we couldn't get a room, we would be able to get whatever Lori needed until she could get her medication.

As we talked, we realized Lori had all kinds of energy, but having left her apartment without her purse, she didn't have any money. Given my disease, I had no energy but had enough money and credit cards. It was at this time we decided to stick together until we could get her to her family and get me out of the city. We went to the hotel/motel and sure enough they had no rooms, but I saw a room open so I thought we could use the phone to contact our families.

Unfortunately, the phone was shut off, but the manager showed us to the office and allowed us to make a call. Since most phone lines were unavailable, I was able to contact my friend in New Jersey and let her know I was ok. My friend, Yvette, agreed to call my mother. She also talked to Lori and got her family's contact information, agreeing to call them and let them know that Lori was ok.

We began hearing that there was a shelter down the street, so we started walking toward the building everyone was pointing to. We finally realized it was a temporary shelter in an apartment complex. We found the recreation area where the apartment manager had set up the shelter. As we got to the entrance, an employee of the complex was taking down everyone's name and contact information. The complex was kind enough to call each person's contact and let him or her know where we were and that we were ok.

We were told the Red Cross would be setting up a permanent shelter sometime later in the day - at this time it was close to 1 pm. The residents of the complex went to their apartments and brought back food and drinks; several tables were set up in the basketball court. The complex had several televisions in the weight room, where most of us congregated to share stories and listen to information on TV. We now knew the Red Cross would be setting up a shelter at some point, but we still didn't know when.

Lori was in need of insulin so the manager agreed to take her to the hospital to see if they could help her there. She was concerned about not having money to pay for the hospital care, so I gave her my credit card and we promised to meet up later. It was much sooner that we thought when the Red Cross opened its shelter, so the manager took me to the hospital to find Lori. Thankfully, she was just about done when we got to the hospital, and the manager took us to the shelter.

It would be the second day, September 13th before Lori would be able to get out of the shelter to meet her husband and before I would be able to get a train to Missouri. The one good thing that came out of my experience was meeting Lori. She and I have remained friends to this day. I thank God for bringing her into my life every day.

ELINDA FISHMAN KISS

A finance professor from Philadelphia
recovers her laptop from the rubble

Elinda Kiss was an associate professor of finance, traveling from Philadelphia, PA to attend the NABE economics conference at the hotel inside the World Trade Center. (She was on the Board of Directors of NABE.) She was staying on the 15th floor of the hotel. Her laptop was miraculously found in the rubble by a firefighter.

"MY PREVIOUS SENSE OF INVULNERABILITY WAS SHATTERED. FOR A LONG TIME, WHEN I SAW PLANES SLOWLY LANDING AS I DROVE PAST AN AIRPORT, I RELIVED SEEING THE PLANE CRASH INTO WORLD TRADE TWO."

Photo of Elinda Kiss taken on the top of the South Tower's observation deck at 2 World Trade Center. This photo was taken on September 9, 2001, only two days before the attack.

ON SEPTEMBER 11, 2001, I was at the NABE (National Association for Business Economics) breakfast meeting in the Marriott World Trade Hotel ballroom when the first plane struck. The hotel was physically between the two towers of 1 and 2 World Trade Center. The lobby of the Marriott was attached to the lobby of North Tower (1 WTC). The towers later collapsed onto the hotel.

I saw the chandeliers shake and heard a large "BOOM." I did not have any idea what it was. I remember Bob (another NABE member) remarking, "I do not recall earthquakes in NYC."

Hotel security entered the ballroom and asked us to exit the hotel through the bar because debris was falling from the front of the hotel building. Once outside, Susan (the NABE executive director) asked if I would help lead others toward the river.

Gary (a fellow NABE Board member) was concerned where his wife was, as she had taken a walk that morning. I offered to return with him to look for her. As we were just across the street from the hotel, we saw the large plane strike the South Tower (2 WTC) in the middle of the building. Until that time I had assumed that the first plane had hit North Tower (1 WTC) by accident.

I instantly thought, "This was done on purpose." I knew we would not get back into the hotel, that it would be cordoned off for the investigation and that we should leave the area and ultimately leave New York.

Before the plane struck the South Tower (2 WTC), I had hoped to return to my hotel room to get my computer that contained my class notes, as well as my brief case, which held diskette backup copies of files. But I realized then that we would not get into the hotel that day.

I never thought that the buildings would fall.

I met up with other conference members and suggested that we head north.

My suggestion that we walk to Penn station in Midtown was met with "It is too far." Hence, I suggested that we walk to the nearest PATH station at Christopher Street (in the Greenwich Village area).

Approximately 17 of us headed north. Along the way, we stopped to use the restrooms on the conference floor of a hotel, a few blocks from the Marriott hotel where we held the NABE conference.

When we did leave, our larger group was reduced to four (Roger, Bernie, Lea and I), who were all from the Philadelphia area.

We walked slowly until a policeman told us that the planes might have contained dangerous gases. Then, we heard a large explosion, which we later learned was the collapse of South Tower (2 WTC)

I thought it was another bomb. We ran - some ran so fast that they ran out of their shoes. Bernie was more than a block ahead of us as he had longer legs than the rest of us.

I suggested that we walk along the west side - close to the Hudson River - so that we could jump in if necessary (it may be polluted but it was warm outside, and if there was a fire, it may have been better to be there).

When we reached Christopher Street, we headed east to the PATH station, only to learn that subways and PATH trains were not running.

It was near the Christopher Street PATH station that we saw the North Tower (1 WTC) fall. From about two miles away, it looked as if the building imploded.

At that point, I suggested that we walk along Hudson Street (which would turn into 8th Avenue), so that when we reached Midtown, we would be closer to the train station and not need to walk across several avenue blocks in Midtown.

When we walked past a beauty shop, I asked the group to wait while I went in to ask if I could use the phone as my cell phone wasn't working (public phone lines at restaurants and hotels were long). As I was dialing my husband's office, my cell phone rang, and a female voice shouted, "Thank God you are all right."

I responded, "Who is this?"

It was my sister, Cheryl, who lives in a Detroit suburb.

Strangely, it never occurred to me that this attack would be news all over the US (and the world). Because I worked in Newark, NJ (just across the river from New York) and New Brunswick (40 miles from NYC) and commuted from Philadelphia to NYC for 4 years (90 miles), I tend to think of NYC and what happens there as local. I assumed that my husband in Philadelphia would not hear of the attacks until he listened to his car radio.

It never occurred to me that my sisters and parents would know about the attack. I asked my sister to call my husband and parents to tell them that I was ok, but that I had not been able to make outgoing cellular calls. For some reason, my cell phone worked inside buildings that day but not outside.

We proceeded slowly toward Midtown, happy to have each other's company. I served as navigator since I had worked in NYC for four years.

Buying sneakers

When we reached Penn station, we learned that trains were not running. I suggested that we eat lunch (a few blocks from Penn station so that crowds would be smaller) since we may not have had the opportunity later. Bernie suggested that we use the restrooms at the hotel across the street. Roger suggested that we stop at a shoe store for Lea to buy sneakers since she had been walking in high heels.

Inside the shoe store, I finally reached my husband, who offered to drive to Hoboken to pick us up if we took the ferry. I asked him to call the university to have the secretary put a sign on my classroom door that

I might be late but that I was trying to hold my class in New Brunswick that night.

After lunch, Bernie suggested that we walk to the ferry, but I suggested that we first see if the trains were running (clearly the NYC authorities wanted us to leave the city, if we could). I also indicated that we could stay with my cousin or a friend in NYC, if we could not leave the city.

When we approached the train station, we were told to go three separate ways for the different trains (LIRR, NJ Transit and Amtrak). We reconnected with Rosemary (another NABE Board Member) and other NABE members near the station.

Lea and Roger headed toward Amtrak, while Bernie and I headed toward NJT. The crowd approaching the station was orderly and polite. Everyone was very nice to one another that day. A stranger gave another NABE member – Gil – a pair of shoes, since he had lost his slippers walking down the stairs of the Marriott as he had been in his hotel room, not at the breakfast, when the first plane hit the North Tower.

Once inside Penn Station, I went to the machine to purchase a ticket and was informed by a NJT employee that the ride was free. Since I knew the NJT trains, I indicated to Bernie at which track we should wait, and we were among the first passengers on the second train to leave NYC that day.

As the train pulled out of the tunnel and into NJ, I looked back at the smoke that was WTC, and was utterly shocked by what had happened.

I arrived at New Brunswick station and took a taxi to the university.

My email simply said, "Elinda is alive."

When I arrived at the university, I learned that classes had been canceled. I decided to go to my office to retrieve cell phone messages from my office phone. There were 22 messages. My husband's first message was one of panic before he knew that I had survived.

There were messages from my parents, sisters, step daughter and even some students who knew that I had been in NYC.

Since my laptop computer was left in WTC, I used my office desktop to read and send emails. There were more than 40 messages from students and friends expressing concern. I responded to my entire address book with an email titled, "Elinda is alive."

I received emails from students whom I had taught in Beijing in August 2001. Since I had lost a suit in the hotel that I had purchased in Beijing, several of my students arranged to buy me a replacement (which I paid for and a colleague brought back to the US for me).

My sister and I had bought identical blouses in Venice; she gave me her blouse to replace mine. The cell phone store replaced my charger for free. In general, everyone I met that week who knew of my experience was quite supportive.

My husband said that "I was like stone" when I returned home that evening. I had remained "calm" to help others leave the area.

The anxiety surfaced on Wednesday as I listened to the radio while I went about trying to replace the possessions that I had lost in WTC. That morning, I called everyone who I knew had been at the conference and was happy to learn that they survived.

I found it helpful to talk about the experience and to be with other members who shared the experience.

Recovery of my laptop

In January, 2002, I received a telephone call from a volunteer fireman who had found my laptop while sifting through the rubble of WTC. He had to turn it over to the police. He noticed that although the laptop sustained substantial fire damage, my university business card was still white. He could read my last name, Kiss, which he remembered. Five years later my laptop was found by a museum employee who used it to curate an exhibit on September 11)

The firefighter called Rutgers University, asking for Professor Kiss. When he reached me, he asked where I had been in WTC, and where my laptop was. I responded that my laptop had been in my hotel room on the 15th floor, but that I had been on the ground floor in the ballroom at breakfast.

He said he found my laptop approximately 60 feet below ground at the site. He said he wanted to speak with a survivor since he had lost 16 friends who were volunteer firemen that had tried to help recover people who had been in WTC.

A volunteer fireman found Elinda's laptop in January 2002.

The laptop was recovered when a firefighter was sifting through the rubble in the World Trade Center. Although the laptop sustained substantial fire damage, the Rutgers business card was readable.

The firefighter remembered the name "Kiss" on the card and called the university and asking for Professor Kiss.

A difficult return to Ground Zero

In April 2002, I returned to the WTC area (now called Ground Zero), accompanied by several students. I was shocked to see that all the WTC buildings were leveled.

I was quite upset to see the devastation.

My husband asked to go see the area in June 2002. At that time, it did not bother me as much to see it as it did in April, but it still is sad and upsetting that so many people lost their lives and that our country has not been the same since. We no longer can simply walk up to or drive past Independence Hall in Philadelphia. So many places now require security clearance.

Everyone's life in the US has been changed, not just the lives of those who survived.

How my life changed

Hearing the explosion and being ushered out of the NABE breakfast on September 11, I never anticipated how our lives would change that day.

I lost possessions (my computer, briefcase, clothes, sundries and suitcase), but most significantly, I lost my class notes, working papers, exams and all the work for the fall semester. Still, possessions can be replaced; I, along with all other NABE members, had my life and physical health in tact.

However, my previous sense of invulnerability was shattered. For a long time, when I saw planes slowly landing as I drove past an airport, I relived seeing the plane crash into the South Tower.

On a more positive note, I believe that the US became a friendlier nation in the wake of this tragedy. We became more concerned about our fellow citizens. Everyone we encountered in NYC on that day was helpful and friendly. NJ Transit did not charge fares as we left NYC. Strangers offered money and shoes to those without. Many of my colleagues stood in three-hour lines to donate blood. We came together as a country, protective of our own.

JAREK KLIMCZAK

A co-worker's mistake saves a Polish-American man from death

Jarek Klimczak, a Polish native, was traveling to New York for business. He was staying in room 1043 inside the hotel of the World Trade Center. Jarek is certain that if his two co-workers had not made the mistake of arriving to the hotel at the wrong time, he would not be alive today. Because of the mistake, Jarek left his room two hours earlier and ultimately escaped. Now, he carries his hotel keycard around with him at all times as a constant reminder of 9/11. Witnessing the attacks has left him shaken to the core.

"ONLY THE HOTEL KEYCARD AND I ARE STILL AROUND FROM ROOM 1043. SOMETIMES, WHEN I AM VISITED BY THE MEMORIES OF THAT DAY, I PULL IT OUT, LOOK AT IT AND WONDER HOW THIS DAY WOULD HAVE TURNED OUT FOR ME IF HARRY AND TONY HAD COME ON TIME."

HUNDREDS OF CHILLING, horrid stories from that Tuesday morning we will never read — these are the accounts of those who perished that day. We read only stories of those who found themselves in the path of destruction but escaped their demise by the grace of pure luck or a combination of smart actions and luck. In my case, it's pure luck - a consequence of a mistake.

Summer 2001 was all about several weeks of work at the offices in London and traveling across Europe, far away from my home in Long Beach, California. I also visited my homeland Poland and received family-related items of profound sentimental value. These items and almost all of my possessions - wardrobe, electronics and photo equipment - traveled with me in three large suitcases.

Eventually after months abroad, I returned to the United States on September 10th. In the late afternoon, I checked into WTC Marriott (room 1043) to get ready for an 11 am meeting the next morning at the Battery Park World Financial Center just across the street.

The jet lag woke me up just in time to see the sunrise. My room faced the east, and from its oversized window offered a stunning view of both towers shooting up into the lucid sky, the rising sun just between the two of them. I got some breakfast delivered to the room, took scores of breathtaking photographs and consumed this mesmerizing view — so magnificent, so tranquil, so hopeful.

My plan was to take a shower around quarter to nine, dress up for business, review my presentation and meet with my team half an hour before 11.

Half an hour before nine, my phone rang. It was Harry and Tony from my team. They were downstairs in the lobby waiting for me. They thought the meeting was at nine. They made a mistake.

I decided to meet them downstairs for coffee before returning to my room and continuing with my plan. I put on my jeans and a polo shirt, grabbed my door key card and went down to the lobby. The idea was to sit down for coffee at the bar at Windows on the World - at the top of Tower One - but at the elevator entrance the staff told us it was closed to the public for some business group meeting. With that, we decided on a coffee bar at the WFC atrium.

Just when we stepped onto the catwalk that crossed over West Street and connected to the atrium, we heard this strange sound, which left us puzzled for a few moments. Unaware that just above us an airliner had crashed into the building we were leaving, we proceeded and ended up outside on the west side of the atrium in front of a little harbor. What I didn't know at the time was that from there, I would become an eyewitness of the surreal horror but not one of its victims.

After the collapse, now from a safer distance standing on West Street, I was looking at the rubble covered with a thick gray cloud of dust. I tried in vain to grasp the depth of human tragedy that had just transpired before my eyes. Anybody who witnessed this had to be fundamentally shaken and left deeply affected forever.

Only hours before, the items in my luggage seemed so dear to me - some of them too precious to ever consider losing. But in the face of this scene of carnage, and in the instant of their disintegration, they all became trivial objects not worth a thought. Articles of clothing, style and fashion, brand names and gadgets no longer attracted me as they did before. Now, I'm left with a passion for art, and through it I search for elusive answers about that day and the irrational nature of fate.

Since that tragic morning, I always carry the WTC hotel keycard with me in my wallet. Only the hotel key card and I are still around from room 1043. Sometimes when I am visited by the memories of that day, I pull it out, look at it and wonder how this day would have turned out for me if Harry and Tony had come on time - two hours later. At the moment of the first impact, I would have been taking a shower then watching the tragedy unfold outside my window. I would have been glued to it—observing, filming and taking pictures of the scene. Even after the second impact, I would have felt perfectly safe in my room, only to be proven tragically wrong at 9:59 am when my room, together with the whole middle section of the hotel, was turned into dust. My story would be chilling and horrid, and like hundreds of other similar accounts, would never have been written.

BERNARD M. MARKSTEIN

A chief economist's close call

Bernard M. Markstein is the President and Chief Economist of Markstein Advisors. On September 11th, 2001, he was traveling from Pennsylvania to New York City to attend the economics conference inside the hotel at the World Trade Center. He was a hotel guest on the 13th floor. Bernard escaped with several other conference attendees on September 11.

"THIS WAS NO ACCIDENT. IT WAS ANGLED DOWN AND HEADING DIRECTLY AT THE TOWER. IT WAS LIKE IN THE MOVIES, ONLY THIS WAS REAL."

My Arrival to NY

I REGULARLY ATTEND THE annual meeting of the National Association for Business Economics (NABE), a group I have been involved with for about 15 years. The meeting, set for September 9 through 11, 2001 was to be held at the World Trade Center Marriott Hotel, a building that sat on the southwest corner of the World Trade Center complex. It was also known as World Trade Center 3, next to World Trade Center 1, the south tower. It was approximately 22 stories high.

My arrival on Sunday was uneventful. I parked my car in a garage near the Trenton train station and took the 10 a.m. New Jersey Transit train to Newark where I changed for the Path train to the World Trade Center. From the Path exit, I proceeded through the lobby of tower 1 (the south tower) to the Marriott Hotel. After picking up my conference materials, I had enough time before the first session (a luncheon meeting) to check into the hotel. I was given a very nice room on the thirteenth floor. I remember being amused that this hotel was willing to ignore general superstition and have a thirteenth floor (many hotels simply jump their numbering, going from 12 to 14, conveniently leaving out a floor numbered 13 which obviously still exists).

Tuesday Morning

Tuesday, September 11, I awoke early enough to dress and pack my bags prior to a breakfast meeting scheduled at 8 a.m. I thought about taking my bags downstairs with me, but decided instead that I would return at the 10 a.m. coffee break, gather my bags, and check out. I headed downstairs carrying only my briefcase. Because I had packed up and was to head out later that day, I had put my car keys in my pocket (I had kept them in my room during the rest of the conference). As usual, I carried my wallet and change. As had been my custom during the conference, I slipped my cell phone into my pocket. (Nancy and I had purchased cell phones for the first time in July, prior to our vacation to Tupper Lake in upstate New York.) I had noted my cell phone charge was low and had plugged it into the recharger for a short time prior to going down to the breakfast meeting.

The BOOM!

After eating breakfast, our speaker, had just been introduced by the chief economist and begun to speak. As we sat there (around 8:45 a.m.), the lights dimmed briefly then came up again. Glass pendants, which were hanging around the lights to give a chandelier like effect, began to tinkle like there was a slight breeze wafting through the room. I remember looking up at them and thinking that it was odd. Then we heard a huge "BOOM!" which seemed to come from the front right of the room (roughly to the northeast by my reckoning).

Was it a bomb?

We all sat for about two seconds. Then a number of people stood up and started heading rapidly for the exit. In short order, all were on their feet, heading for the exit. I remember thinking as I stood up, "World Trade Center, bomb" (there had been a bombing of the World Trade Center in 1993 in which six people died and there was some damage, but otherwise the bombing was unsuccessful as the intention to collapse the building failed). I grabbed my briefcase and headed for the exit along with everyone else. As I approached the exit doors, the emergency alarm was sounding (roughly 10 to 20 seconds after the initial boom).

While people were quick to exit, there did not appear to be any pushing or shoving. Once outside in the main hall, I saw a woman on the floor who had apparently tripped over a tripod holding a placard announcing our event. A number of people surrounded her to protect her from the crowd while one person helped her to her feet and another folded the offending tripod. A few people (five to ten) burst into the corridor from the entrance off the south tower lobby. They were clearly in a panic and running. A number of us turned to them and in a loud voice told them to slow, to walk, and not run. Surprisingly, they did.

People were trying to exit via the hotel's main entrance, which faced west, but came back inside because of falling debris. At that point we did not know what had happened. Looking through the large glass windows next to the hotel's west entrance, I could see cars at odd angles on the street. Had there been a very bad car accident? A gas explosion? A bomb? These were the thoughts that ran through my head.

Trying to find an exit

There was no ready safe exit at that time, so we milled around the lobby. That seemed safe enough for the moment. I tried to call my wife, Nancy, on my cell phone, but couldn't get a call through.

As I was looking for an exit, someone in a work uniform down the hall towards the entrance onto the south tower lobby seemed to be waving us that way, indicating we should exit there. I started towards those doors, got about half way there and noticed that the lobby on the other side of the doors appeared to be filled with smoke. That didn't look like a good way to go, so I turned back, telling the few others who had followed me that I didn't think that was such a smart idea. They, along with the fellow who I thought first indicated that route, turned back to the main lobby.

Most people were still milling around the main lobby. As we were killing time and didn't seem to be in danger at the moment, I thought idly if there might not be time to run up to my room and retrieve my luggage (which was already packed). I looked at the elevators, which as I expected were in their lockdown position—on the first floor with doors open. I abandoned my luggage retrieval idea, which I have to admit was not too smart to begin with. (Although it was a stupid idea, I wasn't so stupid as to consider walking up to my room on the thirteenth floor to get my things.)

A few moments after that, the hotel opened the doors to its restaurant, allowing us to exit to the south, on Liberty street. At this point, roughly five to seven minutes had elapsed since the initial boom.

As we headed out the door, two firemen entered through that door, ordering us to leave the building—in fact, their entrance was impeding our exit. However, a moment later, they must have received an order to go elsewhere, because they turned and headed back out. With them gone, it was easier for us to exit.

On the street

When I emerged on the street, I immediately ran directly to the west. Debris was still falling, though apparently nothing large. I did notice as I ran that a policewoman who was standing in the street directing us away from the building grabbed her arm as if a piece of glass or something hot had struck it.

I was now about a half block to the west of the Marriott Hotel. I could look up and see the north tower in flames. Flames were shooting out of several floors. Those floors were totally engulfed in flames. Someone told us an airplane had struck the tower. We, like most people, thought it was a small airplane or corporate jet that had gotten in trouble. I wondered why the air controllers would allow an airplane to fly so close to Manhattan.

A person in uniform ordered us to move further away. We moved back to near Two World Financial Center, about a block to the west of the Marriott. I tried several times, unsuccessfully, to call Nancy on my cell phone. Again, I couldn't get a line out. As someone pointed out later, several cells for that area were on top of the two World Trade Center towers. No doubt by then the north tower cells were no longer working. People fortunate enough to get a call out on their cell phone were not relinquishing their line.

The horrific scene

We kept looking up at the unbelievable sight. I could barely imagine the horror of what people on those floors were going through.

People in the crowd yelled,

"Look!"

"Oh my God!"

I looked up and saw a person falling. It was more than I cared to see. I did not look up again when similar cries came from the crowd.

A friend I knew through NABE to whom I had been talking suddenly put her head on my shoulder and said with a tremor, "My God Bernie, my daughter used to work up there until a few months ago."

At that point we weren't sure what to do. Would they get the fire under control eventually? Would we then be allowed back into the hotel to retrieve our luggage? It seemed unlikely that our conference would resume.

Realization this was no accident

As we were milling around trying to call out on our cell phones and trying to decide what to do, I must have heard a sound. Other than that initial boom, I don't remember any sounds from that day; I have since been told that this is not unusual for people who go through a traumatic event. I looked up to see a commercial airplane heading directly at the World Trade Center south tower. This was no accident. It was angled down and heading directly at the tower. It was like in the movies, only this was real. It was 9:03 a.m.

I saw the plane hit, the ball of fire erupt from the building where it entered. At this point I realized I might be in danger from falling debris. I turned to run west (along with the rest of the crowd in the street), hesitating momentarily as I contemplated if the covering in front of Two World Financial Center would provide any protection (I decided it would not).

As I ran to the west, towards the river, I realized that it was very open. There was little protection. I spotted a stonewall that stood roughly seven to eight feet high. I ran to it and put my back against it, figuring it provided the most protection I could hope for. After about a minute or so, it became clear that no debris was falling near me, and that I was safe for the moment (I probably never was in danger given where I was). However, it was now obvious that this was not a safe place. I started walking west again and quickly turned south (little choice given the river was in front of me), following the crowd.

David, another WTC hotel guest

At this point I had completely lost contact with anyone I knew from the NABE meeting. I did not recognize anyone around me. I started talking to a gentleman walking alongside me. He had been at the Marriott attending a different conference on the third floor when the first plane struck. His name was David. He was in charge of Human Resources for a firm that employed about 100 people. His firm had an office in midtown Manhattan. He lived in Rhode Island and had been attending an HR conference.

We walked south, discussing what we had experienced and trying to decide what to do. The weather belied the events of the day. It was a beautiful day with a crystal blue sky. Not a cloud was evident. Several times during the day people would remark on how good the weather was, how fortunate we were that it wasn't raining. No doubt the hijackers had picked that day largely because the good weather gave them great visibility for their plan.

At some point, someone told us that the Pentagon had been attacked as well.

Eventually, we were about four or five blocks to the south of the World Trade Center. We were near a mall-like walkway where we could look back and see the two towers on fire. We felt reasonably safe at the time, never considering that the towers might collapse.

There was a bench nearby, by the water, so we sat down to regroup. I had a map of Manhattan in my briefcase. I pulled it out and considered our options. It was clear we were not getting back into the Marriott that day! We needed to figure a way off the island and home. The Path train from the World Trade Center was no longer an option. My plan was to work my way north to another train station and take a train to New Jersey and my car. I was unaware at that time that the trains were not running.

As we sat at the bench and discussed what to do, some people came up to us and asked directions to the ferry (south of us in Battery Park). They just wanted to get off the island. I was able to give them directions.

The call to my wife

About this time my cell phone rang. It was Nancy! A friend, Liz who had been at the NABE convention earlier, but had gone home the day before, had called Nancy to inquire after my safety. Nancy's call came at 9:23 a.m.

Once Nancy got through to me, I was able to tell her I was all right and that I was going to try to get home if I could.

My plan out

My first plan was to go south, swing east, and then turn north, working a giant loop around the World Trade Center. However, the more I thought about it, I realized that would be quite a walk. I decided that it was worth trying to go directly north, staying to the west alongside the river. I would have to pass very close to the World Trade Center towers, but that route would be faster. I figured that if this were unsafe, there would be a police line turning me back. The cost of trying this option would be going about five blocks out of my way.

I pointed out to David that the safer route was the loop to the south and then east. I offered him my map and directions on that route if he preferred it. He chose to stick with me. As it turned out, my northern route would prove to be the safer one. Again, no one at that time (least of all me) thought of the towers collapsing. Most of the people I talked to later who took the south, east, north route got caught in the debris cloud from the south tower collapse.

David and I started north. Along the way, we ran into three people from NABE from the Philadelphia area whom I knew—Roger, Elinda, and Lea. I gave my map to David in case we were separated.

The five of us proceeded north. We did not run into a police line. We were not turned back. Everyone around us was moving to get out of the area.

Eventually, we reached a hotel (the Embassy Suites) about a block or two to the north and west of the north tower. (The hotel was probably part of Four World Financial Center. The entrance faced west, towards the river.) There was a police line there (yellow tape), representing the north-ernmost line at that point. At my suggestion, we stopped in the hotel to use the restrooms. David chose to stay outside and wait for us.

I was surprised that the hotel was still open and appeared to be functioning. Inside there were people lined up to use the public telephones (remember, it was next to impossible to get a cell phone line out). We stopped briefly in the bar where there was a television broadcasting the news. We quickly determined that they had no real information and knew little more than we did. We decided to continue north.

The collapse of the South tower

As we headed for the door, we looked for David, but couldn't find him. About this time, someone who we believe to be a fireman stuck his head in the hotel and told us to get out, the building was collapsing! We ran outside where everyone was running north and we were again told to run, because the building was collapsing.

I ran about two blocks to the north. As had been the case all that morning, people were running, but not in panic. There was no pushing or shoving. People were careful not to run into or hit anyone.

As I looked to my right, I could see a huge cloud of smoke and debris from the collapsed south tower. No debris was falling around me. The buildings to my east (to my right) were protecting us. Also, the wind must have been blowing from west to east. The tower had collapsed at 10 a.m.

I stopped running. Our group (minus David) recollected itself and continued the trek north.

(I found out later that David had tried to wait for us, but that emergency personnel ordered him to move north. That is when he became separated from us. He eventually made it home that night after walking half of Manhattan. He worked his way north, found a phone and called his office. They told him to go to their mid-town office, in the 50s. He walked there only to find the office closed. After some more calls he walked to Brooklyn where a driver met him and drove him home to Rhode Island!)

Sticking together

Our plan was to stick together, go north, and find a train to New Jersey. As we walked north we tried to call, and eventually got through to, a close relative for each person in our party on my and Elinda's cell phones. We reassured them that we were safe and had them call others. Ironically, my attempts to call Nancy and reassure her that I was still safe after the building collapse failed.

As we walked north and talked, I realized I should call my sisters. I reached my sister Janet. I asked them to call her at home and let her know I was safe. I reached my sister Nancy in Chicago. She had known I was in New York, but didn't know I had been at the World Trade Center. I asked her to leave a message on our home answering machine for my wife that I was OK. By now, my partially charged cell phone was getting low on charge, so I wanted to conserve power for later calls. I turned off the phone to save the charge. Thus, Nancy's calls to me couldn't get through.

The collapse of the North Tower

We were now at Canal Street on the West side highway. We had stopped to make some of these calls and collect ourselves. As we prepared to start north again, I glanced to the south. I said to everyone, "Stop! Look!" We turned to see the north tower collapse. (By now we were far enough north to be out of harm's way.) It was an incredible and frightening sight. It suddenly struck me that I had seen numerous emergency vehicles heading south and only a few heading north (I had seen one dust covered "civilian" car head north as well). Many emergency workers must have been hurt or killed in the collapse. Only later was I to learn how horrific the loss of life for all was.

The north tower had collapsed at 10:29 a.m. We continued to walk north, greatly shaken. There was nothing to do but try to get home.

The smoke rising from World Trade Center

We passed people standing on the street watching the "action"—the smoke rising from the World Trade Center and the steady stream of emergency vehicles speeding south and the occasional vehicle going north—and listening to news blaring from car radios. (There would be a car parked, windows down or doors open with the radio on loud, and people clustered around it. I stopped by one briefly when it sounded like a report on the subway, in hopes that we might get some useful information. None was forthcoming—as in the hotel bar—so we proceeded north.) At one point someone in uniform came by and told people to move north because of the danger of chemicals in the air. I suspect this was more an attempt to move people out of the area since we were so far north and there didn't appear to be a wind blowing anything towards us. We were moving north anyway, so the warning didn't matter too much except that it created some additional anxiety in our group.

We were now near our planned objective, the subway station on Christopher Street where Elinda, who was familiar with the New York train and subway system from commuting for about three years, told us we could get a Path train to New Jersey. As we walked east on Christopher Street we stopped a woman to be sure the station we wanted was ahead. She informed us that no trains or subways were running. It looked like we were trapped on the island for the time being.

Roger quite wisely pointed out that Manhattan was a commuting city and that they would have to let the trains and subways start running again sometime. Certainly the authorities didn't want everyone from outside to stay in Manhattan. That would create its own problems.

The quest for sneakers

In the meantime, we decided to continue north to Penn station and see if we could get some information. As we did so, Roger suggested to Lea that she might want to stop and buy some sneakers (she had been wearing high heels since leaving the Marriott; also she had carried her laptop computer which Roger and I took turns carrying early on). Roger had spotted a shoe store in the previous block. Lea agreed that it was a good idea but it wasn't worth going back, surely we would see another shoe store eventually.

The Foot Emporium

A few moments later, Roger pointed across the street and said, "Look, Lea, Foot Emporium. We can get you sneakers there." We pointed out to Roger that his great find was **FOOD** Emporium (an understandable error given that the sign was in a hard to read script where the "d" did look a bit like a "t"). We had a good-natured chuckle at Roger's expense. There seemed to be some hope if we could let a little humor into our thoughts.

News reports had suggested that people stay away from historic and landmark buildings. Fat chance in Manhattan!

Eventually, we reached Penn station. There was a large crowd milling around outside. I went up to one of the police standing in front of an entrance to the station and asked what was happening. He told me that no trains or subways were running and that the bridges and tunnels were closed as well! He did think that the ferries were still running. There was a ferry at 37th and 12th Avenue that would take us to Weehawken, NJ near the Lincoln tunnel.

That didn't seem to help us much, so our group decided to wait awhile and see what developed. We elected to head east and maybe find a place to eat. We went into the hotel across the street from Madison Square Garden. It was utter chaos in there. People were lined up at the desk trying to get a room. The hotel had put out a table with cups, canned soda (long gone), and some ice. We grabbed some cups and filled them with ice. We were all thirsty by then.

Finally getting rid of the heels

Roger and I found a place to sit down while Lea looked for sneakers with Elinda's help. While Roger and I sat and talked, I tried unsuccessfully to call Nancy on my cell phone. An employee asked if she could help us. We explained we were waiting for a friend who was buying shoes. The employee said that was no problem but that if we wanted anything they were closing at 12:45 (it was around 12:15 then).

With Lea now in sneakers and her high heel shoes in a bag, we resumed our pursuit for a place to eat. We soon found a pizza place with an empty table near the door. None of us felt like eating, so we bought some drinks and sat down to figure our next move. Elinda was able to make some calls on her cell phone. We reached Nancy who told us that all of New Jersey transit was closed down—no buses or trains were running! So, even if we got to New Jersey it wasn't clear how we would get to our cars (Elinda's car was in New Brunswick, mine in Trenton, Roger's in Philadelphia at 30th Street station). As best as Nancy could tell, they were letting passenger cars move on the roads. Also, Nancy told us that Philadelphia had closed down the public schools. It began to look like we might be stuck in Manhattan for a while. Elinda noted several times that she had a friend in the area who most likely would be willing to let us stay overnight.

Remembering I had a friend who lived in Elizabeth, New Jersey, I looked in my briefcase and found his telephone number. I suggested that we take the ferry to New Jersey and I would call my friend. If I had the right number (it was an old one) and if he was home (uncertain, but probable), he would undoubtedly give us a ride to New Brunswick to Elinda's car. Elinda would then give us a ride to my car in Trenton. I would take Roger and Lea to Roger's car in Philadelphia. Roger would then take Lea home in Villanova (near where Roger lived). Lea's car had been parked at the World Trade Center and presumably would never be seen again.

Should we take the ferry?

I volunteered to go outside and see if I could find out from someone official if the ferries were still running. I could not find an official, but I saw a bus stopped to pick up people. I figured the bus driver might know something since they had two-way radios on the buses (or so I guessed). I stuck my head in the bus and asked my question. The bus was crowded to bursting with people standing in the aisles. The bus driver didn't seem to know. A passenger said nothing was moving on the west side. But then a number of passengers said that, yes, the ferries were running. Although it wasn't official, they sounded like they knew what they were talking about. I took my report back to the group.

We decided that it was worth a try and started walking to the west, towards the ferry. As we were walking, I noticed a subway entrance with a few people entering and exiting. I stopped a fellow as he emerged from the subway and asked him if the subways were running. He said he wasn't sure about the subways in general, but this line was running on a limited basis. At that point a light bulb went off in each of our heads. We decided to head back to Penn station, just a bit out of our way, and see if the trains were running.

Taking the train instead

When we got there, there was a transit official outside near where the cabs pick up. He told us that the trains weren't running at present but should start to run shortly. He was directing people who wanted to take New Jersey Transit to one entrance and those who wanted to take Amtrak to another. Roger and Lea wanted to take Amtrak while Elinda and I wanted New Jersey Transit. We agreed to split up and hope for the best. (Roger and Lea made it back home safely in record time.)

Elinda and I headed over to the entrance the transit official had indicated. It was the same entrance we had come to when we first arrived in our trek north from the World Trade Center. There was a large crowd waiting patiently outside. Some people filled us in with news reports (a few had radios with them). That was when we first heard that a plane had crashed in western Pennsylvania, supposedly shot down by the US air force (later we learned that that rumor was wrong, that some passengers had fought the hijackers resulting in the plane crashing and presumably preventing it being crashed into another target). We also heard brief accounts of where people had been when the attacks occurred.

After about ten or fifteen minutes, the transit police at the doors opened them and began letting people in. People moved forward—everyone wanted to head home—but there was no pushing or shoving. After letting a group in, the police closed the doors. There was no complaining. Everyone understood that the transit people were doing the best they could under the circumstances.

Getting on our train finally

That was how it proceeded. The police would (presumably) get word a train was on the way, let a group of people into the station, then close the doors again. Eventually, our turn came and Elinda and I went in.

(At one point while we were waiting, we heard air force fighter jets roar overhead. Although I was pretty sure that they were from our air force, I admit to being nervous. I thought in my black humor sort of way, "Great! I walked all the way from the World Trade Center to die at Penn station!")

Once inside, Elinda positioned us equidistant from the entrances to the three most likely tracks our train would be on. We saw two other people from NABE whom we had run into earlier in our walk from the World Trade Center. Thanks to Elinda's positioning, when our train came, we were able to quickly move to a side entrance and get down to the train fast enough to get two seats!

We sat for about ten to fifteen minutes before the train began to move, so presumably anyone who was in the station and wanted to get on the train was able to do so. As the train began to move, everyone applauded.

Talking to other survivors on the train

I was sitting next to a man who worked in the financial district, close to the World Trade Center. He told me the story of his escape. As we emerged from the tunnel on the New Jersey side, he looked back at Manhattan and remarked how strange the view was without the World Trade Center towers! As the train headed south, we were able to see the smoke rising from the area for most of our ride to New Brunswick. At one point on our ride, I put my hand on my head where I found a tiny speck of glass—the only debris that had fallen on me, probably from my initial dash from the Marriott Hotel.

At New Brunswick, Elinda departed. She retrieved her car and then headed to her office at Rutgers University

I arrived in Trenton a little before 4:30 p.m. I called Nancy on my cell phone to tell her where I was and that I would be home in about an hour or so. No trouble getting a cell line here!

When I emerged from the station, two men were selling copies of the "Bucks Country Courier" (a local newspaper) with pictures of the burning World Trade Center towers on the front page. It hadn't taken them long to swing into action.

Heading home

I went over to the garage, retrieved my car, and headed home. I listened to the news in the car on my drive home, trying to get on top of events. Traffic was relatively light since most businesses had closed early and sent their workers home. I pulled up to the King of Prussia exit of the Pennsylvania turnpike, the busiest exit in the entire system, to find no line and even some tollbooths with no cars! Very eerie for a normal rush-hour time. I was home by about 5:45 p.m.

As I pulled in, my family came out to greet me. About the same time, my sister called to check on me. My daughter, Laura handed me the telephone as I got out of the car. I talked briefly to her, and then turned to hugs from the family. I gave them a brief recount of my day. We turned on the television to watch what I had experienced.

Everyone who attended the NABE conference was eventually accounted for. All escaped safely, though some had more traumatic experiences than I did.

Over the next several days, I watched and read the various news reports. I tried to get back to normal, but found it hard to concentrate. The emotions I had not had time to feel began to seep in. Each night I went to sleep with the images of the burning buildings and the crashing airplane in my thoughts. I awoke each morning with the same images. I was a bit nervous each time I heard an airplane fly overhead. (For the first few days, air force planes were patrolling the air space above Philadelphia.) Living only a few miles from Limerick nuclear plant, we are close to a potential target.

We also live under one of the standard approaches to the Philadelphia airport, so planes flying overhead are not unusual.

It was dumb luck I survived

Those people unfortunate enough to talk to me in those first few days heard my story in excruciating detail. Now, over a month later, I am still taking in other people's stories and processing my thoughts and emotions. I learn time and again how truly lucky I was. Most of the decisions I made that day were the right ones, not due to intellect, but due to dumb luck. Well, there's nothing wrong with being lucky.

I continue to grieve and feel sorrow for those who were less fortunate than I.

Two years later

On December 30, 2003, my family and I took a day trip to NYC. This was my first opportunity to return to the WTC site since that fateful day.

For this trip, we left our car in Trenton, took the train to Newark and changed to the Path train to NYC. We went into the WTC station which had been reconstructed and reopened in November 2003. It sat at the same location as the old station which had come up in the center of the complex, between the two towers. Now it came up in the middle of a huge hole since all the debris of the two towers had been removed months before. It was definitely a surreal experience coming up into nothingness. As you came into the station on the train you could see retaining walls with strengthening rods/pipes running through them.

We walked around the site and then retraced some of the path I had taken on 9/11/01. There were changes here and there as buildings that had been damaged or destroyed were repaired or rebuilt. The covering in front of Two World Financial Center which had been a relatively inexpensive Plexiglas/aluminum affair (to the best of my memory at this point—whatever, it had not been very impressive at the time) was replaced with a very nice bridge connecting the two building across the street (Liberty Street) with each other—a red tile affair on the exterior and windows.

First we walked south as I had on 9/11. When we reached the square where I had looked back to see the two burning towers, now there was only empty sky between two buildings. It was very eerie. Then we walked up to a building roughly directly west of the old south tower. We entered a section called Winter Garden, a beautiful glassed in atrium. I was told that the antenna from the south tower of the WTC had destroyed that part of the building on 9/11 and killed many police and fireman. It had since been reconstructed into the atrium.

DONN MONROE

A Detroit man owes his life to a hotel employee

Donn Monroe was inside his hotel room on the 14ᵗʰ floor of the World Trade Center when both planes crashed. He was in his room showering, shaving and getting ready in the midst of the attacks. He was able to leave the building in the nick of time, due to a hotel employee, who diligently went from floor to floor to evacuate guests. The hotel employee subsequently died, when the hotel was destroyed as a result of the collapse of the towers. Donn is indebted to the employee who forced him to leave.

"THE HOTEL EMPLOYEE TOOK ME TO THE STAIRS, TOLD ME TO RUN DOWN AND LEAVE, AND THEN HE WENT BACK SHOUTING FOR MORE GUESTS. THE TIME WAS AROUND 9:35AM"

MY NAME IS Donn Monroe, and I was fortunate to survive the terrorist attack on the World Trade Center. I was in town on business, staying at the Marriott hotel for five days leading up to September 11, 2001. I was due to leave for Detroit that morning and woke at 8am to call my daughter to wish her a happy birthday. I then watched some TV and went to take a shower at around 8:45.

As I was getting into the shower, I heard a loud "BOOM" and the building shook. Being a New York native, I knew there was no history of earthquakes in the area, so I was puzzled. But I went ahead into the shower anyway.

Those of you who were there will remember that the fire alarm sounded shortly after the first blast. I heard this alarm but was covered with soap in the shower. While I was rinsing off, I heard an announcement come over the loud speaker. I could not hear the words over the shower, but I remember that after the announcement, the alarm was turned off.

As a result, I assumed the announcement was to ignore the alarm. So while guests were leaving the hotel, I leisurely left the shower, shaved, brushed my teeth and began ironing clothes and packing for my trip to Detroit.

It was at that time that the second plane blasted into the Towers again. I looked out the window and saw the devastation in the courtyard. I turned on the TV and saw what was happening in the news. But still, I didn't think the towers would fall. So I continued packing my luggage and getting dressed. I called family members to let them know I was ok, and then decided to wait for my limo to arrive at 10:30.

I continued to watch the news until I heard shouting in the hallway.

I opened my door. There was a hotel employee running floor to floor, trying to make sure all guests had evacuated. He told me to leave immediately. I remember a woman opened her door across the hall from me and listened to him, as well. However, she had on her robe and closed her door. She didn't follow me. The hotel employee took me to the stairs, told me to run down and leave, and then he went back shouting for more guests. The time was around 9:35.

I don't know if he made it out because we were on the 14th floor and he still had more floors to go. I went down the stairs and passed a man who believed he pulled a hamstring on the 4th floor. He was heavyset and I couldn't help him alone. So, I told him I would get help.

When I got down to the mezzanine level, there were around 30 firefighters and policemen there. I told them about the man, and some of them ran quickly to get him. They also told me to run from the building. I went outside where a police officer told me to run zig zag across the street. I did so as debris and bodies fell around me.

I started to go south and stopped a cab to take me to the airport. The driver told me the airports were closed and asked if I wanted to go anywhere else. I said no and started to walk further southward while the cab drove beside the South Tower, stuck in traffic.

I took a few pictures of the towers smoking and then heard a loud rumble as the first tower began to fall. That cab was stuck. I was a block away at this point and thought the building was falling over. I figured I was dead and just froze. But the crowd around me starting running, and I got swept up in the crowd. I ran quickly south to Battery Park and was soon engulfed in the smoke.

Two things concerned me immediately: we were obviously under attack, and everyone who was trained in emergency procedures and could lead us just died in that collapse.

So the few hundred of us stranded in Battery Park were on our own. I bellied up to the fence that separated us from the river, put my house keys in my pocket (I still had my luggage, by the way), and waited for the sounds of bombs dropping, at which time I was going to jump in the river and swim for it. The smoke was thick, and it was difficult to breathe. People had taken off their shirts and were breathing through them. A delivery truck driver was opening cases of Dasani water and passing them out, and everyone was sharing the water.

After about 20 minutes, ferries from New Jersey began pulling up to rescue us. I was right in front of the first ferry, and someone helped me climb the fence with my luggage and get on that ferry. As I sat there, noticing that the smoke was dissipating, there was a loud rumble, people started screaming, and the smoke started coming back heavily again. That's when we knew that the second tower had fallen.

The ferry then left for NJ where I walked around, talking to strangers and finally finding a room at a dive hotel (one of those places where rooms are rented by the hour). I remember the person behind the bullet-proof glass at this hotel asking me what I wanted, and when I told her I wanted a room for a day, she turned and asked the other person back there, "How much do we charge for a whole day?"

Anyway, I bought a bottle of champagne and a six-pack of beer from the front desk, turned on the television, and was glued to the news until 3am when I finally forced myself to rest. The next day, I connected with co-workers who also survived the attack, we rented a coach bus (the type used by rock stars), and we traveled back to Dallas on Thursday.

Dedication to Abdu Malahi

After doing some research a year later, I found out that the hotel employee who saved me was Abdu Malahi, a technician who worked for the hotel. The debris from the planes damaged the hotel's intercom system, and the hotel was unable to tell any remaining guests to evacuate the building. Mr. Malahi felt an obligation to get those guests out of the hotel. As a result, he ran floor-to-floor to save those of us who were still in our rooms. He went up several more floors but was killed when the first tower fell on top of the hotel.

*Donn's photo taken from the first ferry to leave Battery
Park, after the second tower just fell.*

Photos taken by Donn Monroe a minute before the first tower fell.

Photos taken by Donn Monroe a minute before the first tower fell.

Unending line of ambulances heading into the tunnel to rescue victims.
"The hotel I stayed at in NJ was at the entrance to the Holland Tunnel. I
was struck by the unending line of ambulances going into the tunnel to help
rescue victims. They went as far as the eye could see. I also remember seeing no
ambulances coming back out. That told me they weren't finding any survivors."

DAVID MURPHY

A sales executive from Chicago desperate to see his family

David Murphy was a Sales Executive traveling to New York City for business on September 11, 2001. He was staying in the hotel inside the World Trade Center and was a guest on the 18th floor. He believes he was in Room 1822. After seeing the horrific scene in New York, he simply wanted to leave and be with his family. He rented the last car from a rental company and drove non-stop to Chicago to be with his wife and kids. David now lives in California and will never forget the kindness of strangers on 9/11.

"I REMEMBER EVERYBODY IN NEW YORK CITY BEING SO HELPFUL. EVERYBODY WAS KIND. EVERYBODY WAS SINCERE."

I WAS IN NEW York City where I had set up a meeting for the next day. I don't spend a whole lot of time in New York City. At the last minute, my hotel was moved to the World Trade Center. I remember checking in late Monday night, the tenth. I believe I even ordered room service and got to bed early because I knew I had a full afternoon the next day. I was going to interview a gentleman, who was a highly skilled sales-person, that morning around 8:45 or 9:00 am.

I was at my desk doing work when the first plane struck. I remember my window almost caved in and hit my face. It was like an explosion. When I looked out my window, I saw debris falling from the top of the roof. I knew right then that I needed to get out of there. I grabbed my phone and shoes with no socks. I put those on. I left my suit and everything else there. I had dress slacks and a belt on.

I went out and looked into the hallway. There were people flowing out of their rooms. At that point, I remember a lady in a robe and a little baby. I remember a guy that had shaving cream on his face. I remember an older couple. I felt bad for them, so I asked them if they needed any help. They said no. I proceeded to go down into the fire escape.

I went down the fire escape. The gentleman I was supposed to interview that morning was getting out of a taxi when the first plane hit. His sister and nephew were in the plane that hit the World Trade Center. He was coming home from New Jersey when he arrived at the World Trade Center and the elevator crashed. As people came out, they were burned. He made the decision to get out of there and went back across the river to New Jersey.

I got out from the fire escape and never saw him that day. He called me later that night, or maybe the next day, or even a week later. I don't know, but I did talk to him a couple of different times.

When I was coming down the stairs, I ran into a gentleman who I had planned to meet because we were going to the same business presentation.

"David, there was a jet that hit the Trade Center tower," he said. "You need to get the heck out of here."

Heeding his advice, I rushed down to the lobby. When I got there, I remember seeing a man with a microphone. He was saying that everything was going to be ok, while people were trampling around in the chaos. I remember trying to find my way to the exit.

There was a large security guard. He said, "No, you need to stay inside...you can't go out 'cause there is debris falling." He didn't forcefully say that, but he said, "I would not go out, because there is debris falling. I thought to myself that I didn't really want to stay in there, though. I was in that room and I heard the noises and smelled the fuel. *I'm getting out of here, right?*

I got out a side exit. I was in the far right room. I went down that far right side, which was where the tower got hit first and went all the way across to the other side. I really didn't know what I was doing, but I somehow got out and I went on the other side of the hotel, away from where the first plane hit. I was standing out on steps and I was looking up in horror, trying to get ahold of my wife to tell her, "Oh my God, it's horrific—a plane accidentally flew into the World Trade Center, and I feel so bad."

Many people were coming out of their office buildings, flowing out. The sirens were going off. There was smoke and the tragic sights of the people jumping off the towers. At first, you didn't know if they were humans that were jumping. People just kept saying, "Oh my God. There are humans falling out of the buildings." Real, live beings were jumping. It was a horrific and scary moment.

The sound that will forever remain is the sound of the jet that's coming down.

While I was looking up, I saw another jet, and it turned sideways. It was literally coming down the street – whose name I don't remember. It crashed into the South Tower right in front of my eyes as I was sitting on the steps of the hotel. Complete chaos took place and I took off to the waterfront.

There were boats out there and I was going to get on a boat but for some reason I thought, "No, I'm not going to get on a boat."

I thought that New York City was being attacked. It was incredibly scary. Instead of boarding a boat, I went all the way down to lower Manhattan.

There, I recognized the gentleman that I had run into in the stairs. He was my partner for probably 30 to 45 minutes. I went to lower Manhattan and walked all the way around the area. We walked all around the area and started coming back up on the other side of Manhattan when the first tower collapsed. Then, the second tower went down. I was quite a distance away and didn't feel threatened.

I stopped at a shoe store and got socks because my feet were killing me. They didn't charge me for my purchase. I remember everybody in New York City being so helpful. Everybody was kind. Everybody was sincere.

I was now headed across the Brooklyn Bridge. I thought to myself that I shouldn't cross that bridge because it could be another target. I wanted to stay away from bridges. I wanted to stay away from high rises. I didn't want to go in the tunnels. Ultimately, I was trying to remain as calm and strong as possible.

I chose not to go across the Brooklyn Bridge at that time. I finally got ahold of my wife and I said that I was okay. She is in Chicago. We were living in Chicago at the time. She was in tears. I had called her the night before and said I was staying at the Marriott World Trade Center Hotel.

I remember the kindness of everyone. Out of pure generosity, a few New Yorkers opened up their apartment to me so I could get water and rest my feet.

At that point, my goal was to find a car and get out of New York City.

I was really nervous then. I went to two rental car agencies, and they were both all sold out. At the next rental, they were all sold out. I went to the third. I think it was 63rd Street thankfully had one more car left, which I rented.

I then proceeded to get out of the city. My wife helped me navigate that late afternoon and early evening. I ended up driving all the way back to Chicago because

I got through the city and got over the bridge and got back to Chicago. I drove all the way, straight through.

I just wanted to be with my family, my wife and kids. That's my story.

Post 9/11

To this day, I struggle with the fact that I didn't stay in New York to help others. I was feeling very selfish at the time; it was all about getting myself out and back to my family. This has been very difficult for me. I've never talked to any counselors about it. It's painful to think that I could have made a difference in other people's lives that day.

It did cross me at that point to help. If anything has bothered me over the years, it's been that.

My heart also aches for the gentleman I was supposed to interview, who lost his sister and nephew on the plane that crashed into the North Tower. Before he safely left the city, he even helped a few folks who had been burned on the last elevator coming down to the lobby of the Marriot hotel.

It probably took me about a year before I started traveling again. I've always been in sales, marketing and design, so I never had any problems with it until 9/11. Time has helped heal the trauma, however, and now fear does not hold me back from traveling. If there's something that's stuck in my heart, it's been the helping piece—of failing to help these people and save lives.

That is my story. God Bless.

JOYCE NG

*A young woman from New England
on a mission to help others*

---

*Joyce Ng was a recent college graduate traveling to New York on
one of her first consulting assignments. She was in Room 1335
at the Marriott World Trade Center hotel. That morning, Joyce
was trapped temporarily inside her hotel room when Flight 11
crashed into the North Tower. The hotel caught on fire and Joyce
had to flee the burning building. The images and sounds from
that day will be forever etched in her memory. Joyce started a
non-profit charity **September 11 Survivors of Three World
Trade Center** to help 9/11 survivors.*

"THE TALL BLOND WOMAN KEPT STOPPING ON EACH
FLOOR TO WARN OTHERS. I ASKED HER WHAT WAS
GOING ON. SHE JUST KEPT SCREAMING, 'GET OUT
OF THE BUILDING!' WE COULDN'T LEAVE THROUGH
THAT DOOR OR WE WOULD HAVE BEEN KILLED BY
THE FALLING DEBRIS"

Room 1335

I WAS ON THE thirteenth floor of the World Trade Center Marriott Hotel when the first plane hit the North Tower. I was getting ready in the hotel room to head for work at 50 Broad Street, a few blocks from the World Trade Center.

It seemed like a regular day on the morning of September 11, 2001. All of a sudden, I heard an immense explosion. The explosion was so powerful, it rocked the building and my entire room shook. I did not know what it was. I thought it might have been an earthquake or a construction accident. I ran out to the hallway to find some news and saw no one.

I called the front desk but all lines were busy. I finally looked out the window. What I saw was unimaginable horror. Fiery debris was raining outside my window. I saw a blizzard of glass, paper, debris and chunks of metal avalanching to the ground into the plaza between the two towers. The explosion had sent burning debris and glass to the plaza below.

I saw scores of people running for cover. I saw other people collapse as they were hit by flying debris. I was shocked and horrified as I watched from my room as people were running for their lives, getting hit by debris and were injured or killed.

More thunderous explosions erupted as additional large chunks of building fell outside my window and came plummeting down to the plaza. Pieces of metal the size of couches fell right in front of my eyes as I looked on in horror. I became terrified that the debris would crash right into my room so I ran to the bathroom. My heart was racing - I thought my life was over.

I heard a woman in the hallway yell, "Get out of the building!" I went out to the hallway and saw a tall blond woman yell, "Get out of here!" Some people started coming out of their rooms, confused. At this point, I still didn't know what was happening but I grabbed my wallet and my phone and went to the nearest stairway. Only a few others followed. The tall blond woman kept stopping on each floor to warn others. I asked her what was going on. She just kept screaming, "Get out of the building!"

I continued my way down the stairs and was the first to reach the lower floor. The only exit was a glass door leading to the plaza. Unfortunately, it lead to the plaza between the Twin Towers where it was still avalanching thick dust, paper, glass shards and metal chunks. We couldn't leave through that door or we would have been killed by the falling debris. Fear consumed me for a few seconds at the thought of not being able to get out of the building. I went back up the stairs. I took a chance and got off the floor which luckily, was the hotel lobby. A security personnel was directing people out. Along with numerous other people, I walked out of the building. The first person I noticed outside was a police officer.

He screamed at us, "Get out of this area and don't look up!"

"Get out of the area and don't look up, get out of the area and don't look up." These words rang in my ears as I walked away. I tried to use my cell phone but all connections were busy. As I crossed the street, I turned around and looked up at the World Trade Center - unspeakable horror loomed above me. Flames were bellowing out from the top floor windows of the first tower. I watched in shock as the World Trade Center burned. It was an inferno.

⤚

I felt a wave of sadness as I realized all the people in those top floors were burning and dying. Then I saw bodies coming out of the windows and falling to the ground. People stopped and stared – they could not peel their eyes away from the scene.

For me, witnessing the carnage in the plaza earlier in addition to the falling bodies from the building was too much to handle. I looked away. I couldn't bear to look anymore at the looming death all around me. I was still in the World Trade Center, right outside the door. As I started to look away, I could see a large plane flying from a distance. For a second, I felt relieved because I thought it was the US Military making its way to rescue the people in the burning tower. Then I heard people wonder why a passenger plane would be flying so low towards the World Trade Center. That was when I heard a deafening crash in the sky - the plane had crashed into the second tower! The ground seemed to shake with the crash. The streets were filled with screams and everyone started running. It felt like the end of the world.

I was scared for my life. I started running and looking frantically for cover. Everyone was running for shelter. They were running behind cars or in buildings. I ran so fast that I dropped my credit cards from my wallet. A man with a British accent picked up my credit cards and ran after me to give them back. I was thinking if we were being attacked, the safest place was to go underground. I knew I needed to get underground.

I ran and ran, sometimes it seemed in circles. I ran until I came to a subway station. I got on the No. 5 train at Bowling Green. Heading inside the train station, I met a man whose eyes were injured. Glass flew in in his eyes. He was in pain and just wanted to go see a doctor to get medical attention.

I hopped onto the first subway that came. The subway had stopped for several minutes to reverse directions. Then the train stopped and would not go any further. Some people knew there was an attack, while others didn't. They started complaining that the train was stopped and they were going to be late for work. I wanted to yell at them, "If you knew what was going on outside, you would NOT be complaining."

However, my nerves were shot. I was shaking too much to utter a word. The train had reversed its direction to go uptown, but then it stopped for several minutes. It was only at that point, in the subway on the No. 5 train going uptown that I found out the World Trade Center was attacked by planes hijacked by terrorists. When the train started again, I got off at the next stop.

I went outside and started wandering the streets of lower Manhattan. I walked around for several hours. I was walking around in a daze. People were setting up makeshift TVs and watching the news from TVs set up on the sidewalk. I was trying to call my family. I was wondering where I was going to go. I was scared to be in New York City. There were rumors that the Empire State Building was attacked and planes were flying everywhere.

It has been three days since this horrific event. It took several hours after the attack for the trembling to stop and my heart to return to a normal rate. I am never going to forget what I saw. The images of carnage and people dying are forever etched in my memory. I have not been able to sleep peacefully without hearing the screams and the explosion and seeing the carnage in my head. I cry when I watch the news. I left behind my luggage in the hotel - it is now covered in the ruins of the World Trade Center collapse. Buried in the rubble are my luggage, clothes, backpack, laptop and notebooks. I lost these items in this horrible event. However, I am grateful that these items are the only thing I lost - I did not lose my life.

I am grateful to the tall blond woman who adamantly went to every floor and yelled for everyone to get out of the building. Without her warnings, I probably would have stayed in my room. I am grateful for the British man in the suit who picked up my credit cards and ran after me to give them back. I am thankful for the hotel who allowed me into their ballroom shelter with the rows of rollaway beds after I was refused by a dozen hotels. I am grateful for the people on 49th street who hugged me and asked if I needed money or help after hearing my story.

Peace to all the survivors. My heart goes out to everyone who has lost or is missing loved ones.

Joyce Ng
9/14/01

Charity Efforts

Since 9/11, I have founded a non-profit charity that helps survivors from Three World Trade Center (or Marriott Hotel). The non-profit charity is called "September 11 Survivors of Three World Trade Center."

Through my charity work, I have had the fortunate opportunity to help many people. I have provided information on resources and programs for 9/11 survivors. I have organized survivor gatherings, including the commemorations every year that brings 9/11 survivors from all over the country. I have also helped foster education by given speeches to schools. I have talked to our nation's leaders and work to help educate others on the impact of that day. Most importantly, I represent the voice of those who moved on but still live with the mental and physical ramifications.

Preserving History

Like many survivors in this group, we kept our hotel room key card as a reminder we escaped. Many of us carried it our wallets for good luck.

For the first few years, I held onto my keycard as a reminder that I was given a second chance to live.

Several organizations contacted me to have my artifacts donated to their museums or exhibits. But it was still very hard to let go of these significant items.

Finally, I knew it was time to let go. I'm glad I did as I think it's in a safer place – at the National September 11 Memorial and Museum. It's also in a place where it will educate others about 9/11 so they know there was a hotel inside the World Trade Center.

Back in the summer of 2001, I was a consultant and traveled to NYC quite frequently for business. The World Trade Center hotel became almost my second home in 2001, as I stayed there frequently for business..

I'll always remember the area around the financial district, the restaurants I used to visit, the park across the street, the chess tournaments played at Liberty Park, and the statue of Doublecheck in the park that was covered in debris after 9/11. I hope my story will provide some insight into the depth of the events that happened 9/11.

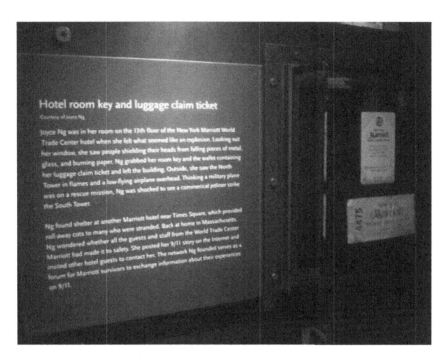

Joyce's Exhibit can be found in the Historical Archive section

ARIS PAPADOPOULOS

Survival propelled him to create a
Disaster Resilience movement

Aris Papadopoulos is a Greek-American from Miami, Florida. On September 11th, he was staying on the 21th floor of the WTC Hotel. Aris was CEO of Titan America, a construction materials company. After escaping this tragedy, Aris sought to give back to society through charity work. He volunteered for the UN Office for Disaster Reduction in 2010. In 2014, he founded a non-profit Resilience Action Fund and wrote the book 'Resilience-The Ultimate Sustainability' (www.buildingresilient.com). He was named Distinguished Expert in Resilience at Florida International University.

"COVERED IN ASH AND DUST, AND BARELY ABLE TO BREATH, THE THOUGHT POUNDING MY MIND WAS 'IS THIS HOW IT ALL ENDS?' I LATER REALIZED MY SURVIVAL MEANT THAT I NEEDED TO DO SOMETHING MORE THAN JUST CREATE AND RUN A SUCCESSFUL BUSINESS."

In the morning

My meeting was scheduled for 9 am on September 11, at the offices of the Port Authority of New York/New Jersey (PANYNJ) on the 65th floor of the WTC North Tower. Titan America, the company I led as CEO, was rene-gotiating the land lease to modernize our Essex cement import terminal at Port Elizabeth, NJ.

I stayed the prior night at the Marriott WTC. Room 2116 looked out at the Hudson River beyond the neighboring World Financial Center (WFC). Above me was the gym with a large indoor pool. On the 19th floor was the concierge lounge available for breakfast and hor d'oeuvres.

Having no prior plans, I went for sushi at Nobu in Tribeca. With a clear night and light crisp air, I strolled back along the river walk. The marina in front of the WFC was quiet. I stopped and lay on a low concrete wall to enjoy the evening peace. Tilting my head backwards and looking at the lit WTC towers, I told myself how beautiful the whole setting was and how lucky I was to be there. It was the perfect calm before the unex-pected storm.

Next morning Takis, Essex VP (15 years my senior), drove in from NJ. A little after 8am, we met at the concierge lounge for breakfast. I carried my notebook, planning to return after our meeting for my briefcase and garment bag. Takis would later drop me off at Newark airport so I could fly to our Norfolk, VA head office.

Always punctual, around 9:40am I signaled that we get going. We had to go down to the hotel lobby, walk to the connecting North Tower, pass security and go up the elevators. Takis, an avid coffee drinker (I prefer tea), begged for time to finish his cup and I acquiesced. As we kept talking an explosion shook the entire building.

Looking out the window, I saw a big black circle on the west side of the North Tower reflecting in the WFC windows. I thought 'bomb!' *(Weeks later I recalled the distinct sound of jet engines in the seconds just before the explosion)*

The 20lb briefcase

The fire alarm sounded. In the hallway windows near the elevators I saw thousands of papers raining down the WTC plaza. We proceeded north towards the emergency stairway. There were few people, as most guests had started their day. Upon entered the stairwell, I told Takis I wanted to go up two floors to get my passport and tickets since I was returning home to Greece in a few days.

He nodded he would wait. As I ran up a woman coming down shouted "don't go up!", but I was already there. *(Later learned that the Boeing 767 front wheel spun off the plane, crashed through the hotel roof and landed in the gymn pool, above my room)*

I sensed this was serious. I rushed to my room, grabbed my oversize hard briefcase (fully weighing 20 lb.) and shoved into it everything on the desk.

Conscious of Takis waiting, I left my clothes and garment bag, ran back out the hallway and down the stairs. We met no delay descending 16 stories, until a hotel person stopped us on the 3rd floor and directed us down the hall to another stairwell at the hotel's south end. From there we reached the hotel's Tall Ships Bar & Grill and its doors facing south. *(Later learned that much of the plane's jet fuel drained down the N. Tower's elevator shafts and flash exploded in the lobby that extended into the hotel, killing and burning many people)*

I could see debris outside the doors. A policeman waved us to cross Liberty St. I raised the briefcase over my head and ran across with Takis. Before me was the backside of St Nicholas Greek Orthodox Church in a brick townhouse dating from 1832, surrounded by parking. I had attended its Sunday services many times. The chapel was barely 1000 square feet with a small parish. *(One was composer/singer Yanni, who donned a psaltis' robe and chanted to accompany the priest. The church was destroyed in the S. Tower collapse and is being beautifully rebuilt. Exactly one month earlier I had visited for my first time ever the holiest of Greek icons, the miraculous Virgin of Tinos Island, at my religious mother's insistence)*

I made my cross as we moved to the far corner of Liberty and West St. Turning we could now see the SW side of a burning N. Tower. In the surrounding voices I heard 'plane hit tower', but only imagined a small plane.

Takis wanted to call PANYNJ to tell them we weren't coming, but I replied they were not waiting for us and were likely evacuating. I motioned we move further away toward the river. Having early in my career worked on oil platforms and refineries, I feared projectiles that fire-related explosions might send our way. We rushed towards the WFC marina and south along river Esplanade. I still wore my jacket, but took off my tie.

In horror we could see human forms jumping from the tower. I asked myself several times if I was dreaming, and if all this could be really happening. 15 minutes after the initial explosion, at the level of Rector Place, I saw a plane flying from the south. As several helicopters hovered the area, my initial thought was of a commercial plane from Newark approaching for a closer view. When it kept coming I said "Where is that pilot going?" As it crashed into the South Tower, I realized this was not an accident.

Someone shouted, "The enemy is attacking. Where is our Air Force?" I thought, 'What enemy? I saw a commercial tail. Have the pilots gone crazy?' I remembered the Egypt Air pilot who committed suicide after taking off from JFK with an entire planeload in 1999.

Running away

In the ensuing panic, I shouted "Takis run!", and started running with my 20lb. briefcase southward along the riverfront. In the commotion I lost Takis. Stopping next to the Jewish Museum, someone urged me to keep moving, "If it's a terrorist attack, this site could be next!" Soon I reached the end of West Street and beginning of Battery Park. Against a clear blue sky and brisk northern breeze I could see both towers burning. Where was Takis? Cell lines were jammed. I got up on a pedestal to look, but could not find him. There I also heard from someone that the Pentagon had been hit.

When the South Tower began to collapse, the smoke, dust and ash reached me in minutes.

People were running in different directions. With briefcase in hand, I ran along the park riverfront, where the Statue of Liberty tours start. Some were trying to get through a construction obstacle. What impressed me was that even in panic, people were courteous to each other. But the smoke and ash was getting too thick to breath. I pulled my shirt up over my nose and mouth. I could not see far and considered dumping the briefcase and jumping into the river to swim. I opened it and shoved my passport into my jacket pocket. I wondered if my remaining life would be a matter of minutes or seconds. The thought pounding my mind was 'Is this how it all ends?'

People rushed into any open cars they could find. At the park's end I saw a few people huddled at a building back door. When it opened, I rushed in with them to the kitchen of the American Grill Restaurant. A few minutes after washing my face at the kitchen sink the water turned brown, as somewhere pipes had broken. I stayed in the restaurant through the N. Tower collapse. My constant thought was, 'Where is Takis?', as phones were still jammed. Able to use my cell as a laptop modem, I read of the crashes and collapses. I connected with my secretary in Norfolk and asked her to let my family in Greece know I was fine.

The evacuation

After the air cleared for the second time, police entered and ordered us to evacuate. I got on a small boat to NJ. Crossing the Hudson I saw smoke where the towers once stood. I continued trying to reach Takis. On the NJ side responders were well organized. I was dusty, but not injured, and walked to the Grand Banks Café a few blocks away. From a pay phone I got Takis' cell messages: OK and crossing over by boat. I met him at the pier. After the 2nd attack he headed north towards his parked car, stopped at the bathroom of a bar and stayed there until evacuated. (*The collapsing N. Tower totaled his parked car*).

An Essex employee picked us up and we drove south. At Edison, NJ I rented a car from Avis. I drove all night to our headquarters in Norfolk and early next morning gathered employees to describe what I had seen. I ended by saying we would commit to rebuilding what had been destroyed.

Six months later we met the PANYNJ officers who had both survived and concluded the agreement to modernize the terminal. Proud that today our materials are in the new Freedom Tower, and that we are donating cement to reconstruct the destroyed St Nicolas Church.

My baggage tag recovered from the rubble

A year and half later, I received a letter from British Air with an attached note from NYPD inviting me to pick up something at their downtown station. They produced in a clear plastic envelope my BA baggage tag that had been found in the hotel remains and traced by number back to me.

I opened it a year later and its touch sent an electric current down my spine. I had my hotel checkout statement (the briefcase), room key and even a chocolate wrapper with the WTC image. All are now framed inside a WTC poster on display in my office.

Takis retired a few years later and at his party got a crystal coffee mug with the towers etched on it. I got a duplicate. His coffee delay likely saved our lives. But in the interlocking of both our fates, my presence that morning had saved his life, because whenever he met with PANYNJ alone he would first stop for coffee at the top of the North Tower. No one from there survived.

The question 'Is this how it all ends?' rattled my mind for months. I decided there was a greater purpose to my life: to build a business based on values and to dedicate myself to the prevention of disasters. I created an in-house values leadership program taught by executives.

The pursuit of disaster resilience

Several years later I became involved in the UN International Strategy for Disaster Reduction (UNISDR), serving as chair of its Private Sector Advisory Group 2011-13, which evolved into the current UNISDR ARISE program. I participated in the drafting and signing of the UN's Sendai Framework, a milestone international agreement on disaster risk reduction. I also served on the board of CTL Group, one of the primary technical investigators of the WTC towers' collapse, and as an engineer studied the buildings' failure.

In 2014, I retired as CEO to dedicate myself to disaster resilience, founded the non-profit Resilience Action Fund, dedicated to awareness, transparency and education for a stronger and safer built environment and published a related book (www.buildingresilient.com). In 2015, I was named 'Distinguished Expert in Resilience' at Florida International University's Extreme Events Institute and helped establish the first graduate certificate in Urban Disaster Resilience.

My aim, with God's love, is to create for future generations a built environment that is stronger and safer against disaster hazards.

SCOTT PASKEWITZ

*An Engine 58 firefighter rushes into the Marriott
Hotel to save others and was caught in the collapse*

---

*Scott Paskewitz was a Firefighter in Engine Company 58
located in Harlem on 5ᵗʰ Ave and 113 Street. On September
11ᵗʰ, he was 29 years old. He with other firemen ran rushed
into the hotel's lobby in the World Trade Center to help. When
the hotel collapsed, he was thrown to the grown and thought he
was dead. Scott went back into the collapsed to search for others,
including their Lieutenant, Robert Nagel. On 9/11, Engine 58
lost Lt Nagel from the attacks. For Scott and the firefighters who
survived, the horrors of 9/11 never go away. It is something they
carry with them every day.*

"AFTER FLYING THROUGH THE AIR, FOR WHAT MUST
HAVE BEEN A FEW YARDS, I LANDED ON THE GROUND
AND THE RUSH OF AIR BEGAN TO SUBSIDE. IT WAS
STILL SO DARK YOU COULD NOT SEE YOUR HAND
IN FRONT OF YOUR FACE IT WAS VERY DIFFICULT TO
BREATH BECAUSE OF ALL THE DEBRIS IN THE AIR."

WORKING ON THAT day in Engine 58 were: Lt Robert Nagel, Firefighters John Wilson, Mike Fitzpatrick, Scott Paskewitz, Pete Giammarino, Dave McGovern, John Weber, and Andy Ansbro.

On 9/11/01 I came into work early, as was my usual routine. I wanted to get some studying done for the upcoming lieutenant's exam. I vividly remember driving in that day because of what beautiful weather it was, not a cloud in the sky. After getting ready for the tour, I grabbed a cup of coffee and headed off to a study room that we had in the firehouse.

I remember being aware of the time because I needed to wrap things up and get downstairs for the start of the tour at 9AM. Just as I was doing so I heard an announcement over the firehouse PA system from one of the guys downstairs that a plane had hit the World Trade Center. I had to find to find a TV to take a look. I walked next door to one of the company offices and saw smoke billowing out of one of the towers. I went downstairs to watch with the other guys. We all assumed that it was a small plane that had accidentally crashed. There was a lot of announcements over the PA system by the Manhattan dispatcher instructing units who were going to the fire.

As we watched both units, Engine 58 and Ladder 26, members wondered if either of us would be sent. As we watched it seemed so unbelievable when a commercial jet flew right into the other tower on live TV. This was the first time that we all realized that this was not an accident. I recall it being less than a minute before we heard our company, Engine 58, called out by the dispatcher to respond to the 5th Alarm for 2 WTC, or the South Tower. I remember getting the adrenaline rush that came along with knowing you were going to a fire. This rush was somewhat tempered by Lt. Nagel, a 28 year FDNY veteran when he said "exactly what I need a 110 story walk up". This made me realize that this was going to be unchartered territory trying to put out 2 fires of this magnitude.

As we responded the streets were not very crowded and we were making good timing getting from our firehouse on 113th St and 5th Ave in Harlem all the way downtown. I remember when we were turning onto the West Side Highway that there were police officers with their guns drawn directing traffic. We went down the West Side Highway as far as we could because it was blocked by all the other fire apparatus that had responded earlier. As we got out and started to grab our gear Lt Nagel reminded us to take our time and grab everything because we were in for a long day. He also insisted that we stay together.

We began to walk south together on the East Side of the highway. I remember only walking a short distance before hearing really loud banging like shotgun blasts. As we got closer, those sounds turned out to be the bodies of people trapped above the fire who were jumping and hitting the ground. We had to watch their falls so that we could avoid being hit. As we moved past the North Tower the sound was almost deafening. It didn't seem real because after impact there was almost nothing left.

When we got to the corner of Liberty St and West St we made a left onto Liberty Street in hopes of finding the Command Post for the South tower. As we turned and headed east on Liberty St. we ran into Engine Company 216 who were carrying one of their members, Dan Suhr, who had been hit by a jumper. We helped them as they moved him across Liberty St away from the building and the danger of someone else suffering the same fate. Once out of what we all thought was harm's way we started to look for the Command Post, which is where we would get an assignment. Someone told us that there were some chiefs in the lobby of the Marriott Hotel. We entered the Hotel through the restaurant, Tall Ships *Tall Ships*, which was connected to the lobby of the hotel.

Once inside the lobby Lt Nagel told us to put our equipment down and he would go speak to the chiefs about an assignment. As he walked North in the lobby toward the chiefs, who were near the front desk, I could see that 2 of them were from our Battalion, 12, Chiefs Fred Scheffold and Joe Marchbanks. It was only a minute or 2 two when a loud sound began to echo through the lobby, getting louder and louder, almost like a train entering a subway station. Then looking through the Lobby Windows it began to get pitch black and the ground began to shake. Someone yelled get away from the windows. Everyone started to run south back toward where we came in.

After a few steps there was a gust of wind and debris that launched me into the air. After flying through the air, for what must have been a few yards, I landed on the ground and the rush of air began to subside. It was still so dark, you could not see your hand in front of your face It was very difficult to breath because of all the debris in the air. Very slowly it began to get a little brighter and people began to move around the lobby. There was a large mass of rubble blocking the path back to the middle of the lobby so the only way to exit was through Tall Ships.

As I made my way to the exit, people were having a hard time getting out. I made my way to the front and realized that the roll down gate they used to close the bar off from the lobby had come down. I grabbed the bottom of the gate with another person and we lifted it up. People began to exit and I realized that the other person lifting the gate was Firefighter Mike Fitzpatrick. We took a few steps towards the exit when we realized that the other guys from our company weren't with us so we decided to take a look back in the lobby for them.

When we went back toward the pile of rubble we came across Firefighter John Wilson. He said that Lt Nagel was trapped but he could speak to him. As we got closer we could speak to him and were able to pass him a flashlight. The pile was very unstable so we needed to be very careful so as not to cause any shifting and further injure Lt Nagel, or ourselves. Also in the lobby was Deputy Chief Thomas Galvin, who was from the 3rd division, which is where E58 is located. Chief Galvin had us tie search rope around a huge pillar in the lobby and leave the rope as close to Lt Nagel's current position so in case of further collapse or shifting. Chief Galvin had to leave to find the command post and coordinate the operations but said he would send in a unit to assist us. While waiting we could speak to Lt Nagel and he said he was in a tight spot but was OK. He said he could hear people further behind him in the c and they were in bad shape. He knew that John, Mike and myself were OK but was concerned with the other four members. We told him that they had gotten out and were Ok but really we had no idea. T Lt. Bob Nagel was the type of leader always concerned about his men before himself.

We decided that we needed some tools if we were going to rescue Lt Nagel. I was on my way outside to see what I could find when I ran into Ladder 113. I led them back inside. Chief Galvin told them that Lt Nagel was trapped and Lt Ray Brown of Ladder 113 was now in charge of helping to get him out. The members of Ladder 113 had some tools but I figured we could use whatever we could get so I went out to see what I could find.

As I exited the hotel through the bar I could not believe what I saw. It looked like what I would imagine a post nuclear landscape. There was grey ash and soot all over and the sun that shone so brightly earlier was barely penetrating the debris filled air. I looked up over my shoulder to where the south tower stood before I entered the building It was gone. A thick grey dust cloud now filled the air where a 110 story building once stood. This was the first time I realized that the building had collapsed and I was some-how still alive. There were crushed fire department vehicles all over the street. I was able to find one that I could get a door open, In the compart-ment was a gas powered saw. I grabbed it and started to head back to the building. As I was a few feet away from the building a large piece of piping came crashing down right next to me. I hurried back inside thinking that must have been a safer place.

When I got back inside I told Mike Fitzpatrick that the tower had col-lapsed and was gone. He told me I was crazy. There was no way that could be. If that had happened we would not be alive. I was adamant about it and he took my word for it.

Lt Brown made a plan to get to work trying to remove the debris and free Lt Nagel. Mike was going to use a saw to cut away the metal. Lt Brown held the flash light to direct Mike where to cut. The rest of us had to watch to make sure nothing shifted. If something shifted unexpectedly we had to warn them to dive out of the way. The operation was not underway long when I began to hear the same roaring noise and air rush that I heard when the south tower collapsed. Unlike the 1st time, this time I knew exactly what was happening, the North tower was going down. I began to run and again after a few steps was thrown through the air. I remember thinking that I was lucky to survive this once and was surely going to die this time. I was shocked when I landed and nothing fell on top of me. The rushing air subsided like before and all that remained was darkness and thick choking air. There was a hissing sound as I lay there. I recall thinking it might be a gas leak. Luckily it was only a leaking air tank from a firefighters' gear. d I was able to shut it off.

As I made my way to my feet I looked to see if Mike and John were

OK. I found John first and he was OK. When we found Mike he had hurt his leg and was hobbling. Even worse off was Lt Brown who was very banged up and could barely walk. We looked to see if we could find Lt Nagel.. There was a lot more debris in front of where he was and we couldn't hear him when we called out to him, with and without the radio. The search rope that we had placed by him had disappeared into a pile of rubble. We realized that we needed to get help if we were going to rescue him. We decided that we needed to get out and regroup.

This was going to be no easy task as the exit through the bar no longer existed, having been crushed by the collapse. The only way out was to climb on twisted beams that came up out of the ground through what was West St. I recall it being about a two story climb up out of the building. Mike was having a hard time with his injury. Ladder 113 had to nearly carry Lt Brown. There were some fireman calling out to us as we climbed out. They had survived on the small section of floors, above the lobby that still remained in the hotel.

As vivid as many of the memories inside the hotel remain after we escaped, the exact timing and sequence of things gets very jumbled. I recall Mike going in an ambulance to have his injuries checked out. I walked west thinking that if we could get near the Hudson River that would be a safe place to regroup. I tried to use my cell phone to call home but couldn't get service. As I walked I saw a police officer and asked if I could borrow his phone. I can only imagine what I looked like because he looked at me like he saw a ghost and let me use his phone. I called my wife and all I remember saying that I was alive. She had no idea that I was at the WTC being that my firehouse was in Harlem. Once, I got to the river we met up with the other guys from my company, Dave, Pete, John and Andy. They had all escaped after the 1st collapse and we were all OK except for Lt Nagel. They said that there were radio transmissions saying we were all dead. It was so chaotic that you couldn't even get through to respond and correct the misinformation. It wasn't until we were able to find Captain John Newell of E58 that it was cleared up. In fact all members of E58 were accounted for except Lt Nagel.

Captain Newell gathered a bunch of our members. John and I took them back to the section of the lobby that we last had communication with

Lt Nagel. We showed them the search rope and explained that we could speak to him before the 2nd collapse. There were a lot of firefighters in there and they were trying to formulate a plan. I am not sure of how long we were in there before we were all forced to evacuate the building due to fear that the small section that remained would collapse. I remember standing in the street waiting hours for the opportunity to go back in to search. It was late in the day and 7 WTC had just collapsed when I decided that I needed to go to the hospital to have my eyes looked at. My eyes were burning and irritated all day and I had corneal abrasions form the debris that was trapped in them.

This is both a story of survival and loss.

There were 7 firefighters in Engine 58 lucky enough to survive but tragically Lt Robert Nagel did not. This is also a story about the randomness of who died and who survived that day. All of us were in the same area.

As I remember it after 14 years have passed, and certainly some of the details could be remembered differently, , the major events of that day are still very fresh in my mind.

I want the story of Lt Robert Nagel and Engine 58 to always be remembered.

ANULFO PONCE
The hotel's chief engineer helps others

Anulfo Ponce was the chief building engineer at the hotel inside the World Trade Center. He and Greg, another engineer, were able to help many guests evacuate the hotel. They assisted one guest with multiple sclerosis trapped on the fifth floor, and were reunited with the disabled woman and her mother eight years later in Chicago.

"THE PURPOSE TO ALL OF THIS IS TO SHARE AN EXPERIENCE WITH WONDERFUL PEOPLE THAT NEVER WERE PART OF MY LIFE BEFORE. I NOW CONSIDER THEM FAMILY, AND I GUESS THAT'S WHAT I GOT FROM THIS EXPERIENCE"

I WAS THE CHIEF building engineer. I got all of the complaints from hotel guests. I remember that day very well. It was a beautiful, clear, sunny morning. I had just met with Leigh and Faye, her mother, in their hotel room. Leigh was disabled and we were helping her set up.

The woman in the wheelchair

Leigh was in a wheelchair and had tried to get into the shower and accidentally pulled the handle out of the wall. She was very upset because she almost fell out of the chair in the shower. It was the type that you sit - not slide - on and it was very shaky. In light of Leigh's complaint, I went to her room on the day before 9/11. I made special arrangements for her and her mother to move to a different floor.

The morning of 9/11

On the morning of 9/11, we had a meeting at 8 o'clock before the first plane hit. There, I pulled Greg aside to tell him to check the room I was going to move Leigh and Faye into. I wanted to ensure that the new room was 100 percent perfect.

I explained to Greg that we needed to check the handle bar in the shower so she could slide over from the wheelchair to the shower chair.

After the meeting, we felt the shake. Something heavy hit and we wondered if it was a truck underneath or above us that dropped a heavy load.

The whole building shook and I said, "Wow! What was that?"

About 10 minutes later, all the alarms went off.

Whenever there is an alarm, we respond to a fire command in the lobby and a dispatch is sent to the fire department. As we all scattered, I went up to the lobby and noticed complete chaos. There was smoke coming from the North Tower, and I said to myself, "What is going on?"

I looked outside the window. There were papers flying and debris falling and chaos.

We had a security guard from the Port Authority directing people not to go outside. Because I am the chief engineer, I walked outside and told the guard, "You know I have to see what's going on. I have to address my building."

When I looked up, I saw huge crater in the North Tower. I went across the street to protect myself from falling debris. I tried to use my phone, but it didn't work. There was nothing that we could actually do, so I went back into the building to make a phone call to my loved ones.

Suddenly, I saw the second plane hit. It was almost right on top of me. From then on, it was just total chaos.

Saving Leigh

Greg was the true hero because he remembered where Leigh's room was. He went up to the room with a fire key and the freight elevator because he knew that the women wouldn't be able to get down to the lobby alone. In the end, he brought Faye, Leigh and another guest to safety.

The second tower went down and we never knew what happened until we saw the documentary of 9/11. I contacted Leigh and Faye, and we've shared a friendship ever since.

They have become our family. That's the whole story.

Reuniting with Leigh years later

Greg and I have met Leigh and Faye. We went to Chicago when they invited us to visit them. They called it a 9/11 reunion. It was all hugs and kisses.

This was the greatest experience of in my life. I was fortunate enough to see Leigh alive again before she passed away from natural causes. Faye is still with us and comes to see us every year. We have an annual reunion. We all have become part of a pack and share feelings with the whole family.

How 9/11 changed my life

We lost two colleagues on 9/11, who we will always remember. It's a hard subject to relive. I guess it is good to remember, but sometimes you also have to understand that the pain keeps getting deeper and deeper.

The purpose of all of this is to share an experience with wonderful people that never were part of my life before. I now consider them family, and I guess that's what I got from this experience.

Further reflections on 9/11

If I would have started walking a little sooner to make the phone call, I probably would have been inside the building and not have known what was happening. You never know how things could have turned out. They could have been much different for me. I believe that I am fortunate to be here. If I would have gone five minutes before, I would not have seen the second plane hit. That's what I keep remembering. I suppose I could have been caught in the middle of it all and I wouldn't have made it out.

Sometimes it's painful to go back, but when you start talking about it, you feel that it's great to remember. Still, after recalling the whole experience, you try to forget the pain. It's good and bad, and sometimes it's just like *holy cow*. You are trying to forget, but you don't want to forget. You are fighting both things at once.

Lessons learned about life

I think ever since 9/11, I take a different approach to life. I used to be very uptight, very work- oriented and more impatient. After 9/11, I learned to put those things aside because I know that life can end in an instant. There's no reason to fuss about materials things. Work is work. You do your best and you don't ruin your life over it because there is so much more to life. We all have to do it, but you don't have to get sick over it.

I think that's what I learned after 9/11.

My boss still thinks I'm pretty uptight, but I find myself not owning that title like I used to. I let things fly now. I got a second chance to live and that's what 9/11 did for me, and now I try to enjoy every day to the fullest. I teach a spin class. I still go to work. I visit my friends and family. I constantly keep reminding myself what is really important in life.

Anulfo Ponce (left) and Greg (right) travel to Chicago to reunite with Leigh (center)

Frank C. Razzano

A lawyer gets buried in the rubble
and is rescued by a firefighter.

Frank Razzano was a laywer from DC who was inside his hotel room on the 19th floor when the towers collapsed onto the hotel. He winded up being buried in the rubble inside the hotel. Frank was rescued by Fireman Jeff Johnson who led three survivors to safety using a rug and finding a hole in the wall to escape. Frank remains forever indebted to the firefighter who saved his life.

"ONLY A FEW FEET FURTHER DOWN THE HALLWAY THE CENTER PORTION OF THE BUILDING HAD COLLAPSED UNDER THE WEIGHT OF THE SOUTH TOWER FALLING DOWN UPON IT... THEN WE BEGAN TO COUGH VIOLENTLY AS THE SOOT, DUST, AND CONCRETE BEGAN TO FILL OUR NOSES, MOUTHS, EARS, AND LUNGS. IT WAS ALMOST LIKE DROWNING. YOU TRIED TO TAKE IN AIR, BUT ONLY MANAGED TO TAKE IN DIRT AND ASBESTOS....FIREFIGHTER JEFF FOUND A SMALL HOLE IN THE WALL ON THE WEST STREET SIDE OF THE ROOM AND FISHED A RUG FROM THE DEBRIS, WHICH HE LODGED IN CHUNKS OF

CONCRETE AND THREW IT OVER THE SIDE OF WHAT
REMAINED OF THE BUILDING AND ANNOUNCED,
'THIS IS THE WAY OUT.' "

Introduction

THE FOLLOWING IS an account of how I survived the attack on the World Trade Center on September 11, 2001, America's second bloodiest day. Some of you who read this may conclude that I am incredibly stupid or incredibly lucky; and some of you will perhaps say his time was not yet up. I prefer to believe the story my mother told me when I got out of the hospital on September 13, 2001. In my early teens, there was a time when each morning I would walk about a mile and a half to a local hospital in Queens, New York to help a priest stricken with multiple sclerosis say Mass. My mother claims that priest repaid me on September 11, 2001 for my kindness. As you read this story, judge for yourself whether my survival was dumb luck or a sheer miracle.

As I write these words, I feel a special kinship with those Americans who survived the Battle of Sharpsburg, as it was known in the South, and the Battle of Antietam, as it is known in the North, on September 17, 1862, America's bloodiest day. Some survived that day through luck, some through stupidity, and some others through miracles. But, whether they were Northerners or Southerners, they were Americans first! And, in the years following the Civil War, they built a nation which, in the last century, became the world's salvation. As I tell this story, I pray that the 9/11 tragedy will reinforce our bonds as one nation, and lead us on to new horizons free of hate and full of love for one another.

The Story

I am a lawyer practicing in Washington, D.C., for the last thirty-eight years. On Monday, September 10, 2001, I was at the law offices located at 125 Broad Street, near the East River in Lower Manhattan, with a partner at that firm, a consultant, and an expert accounting witness who we were preparing for a pending case.

We had worked until 11:30 p.m., but had not finished. We agreed to assemble again the next day at 12:00 noon. Our expert had another meeting the next morning, and the other lawyer had a doctor's appointment. I intended to sleep in on Tuesday, September 11.

Before retiring for the evening, I had a light supper at Morton's on West Street, one block from the World Trade Center. Afterwards, I went back to the Marriott World Trade Center, which was situated directly between the North and the South Towers of the World Trade Center. The hotel was physically connected to the North Tower, and separated from the South Tower by a narrow staircase leading up to the World Trade Center's central plaza where there was a large golden globe in the center of that plaza, surrounded by the World Trade Center complex.

I normally stayed at this hotel when in lower Manhattan as it is a convenient walk to the federal and state courts, and the various law firms in the vicinity of Wall Street. It also had a great gym on its top floor with an Olympic-size pool. I stayed there so often, in fact, the doorman knew my name. On this trip, I had a suite of rooms on the nineteenth floor of the hotel with a living room area, dining room and separate bedroom. I was preparing for an upcoming trial and was using the suite as a "war room," and had boxes and litigation bags on the floor and tables scattered around the suite.

On the morning of September 11, 2001, I was lying in bed sleeping when I heard a whooshing sound and a loud bang. I got up and looked out my window and saw papers fluttering to the ground. Because I had stayed at this hotel many times and had on many occasions heard the winds whistling through the buildings in the World Trade Center complex, I assumed that a freak wind had blown out a window, causing the rain shower of papers descending to the ground outside my window. Although it occurred to me that such a freak wind would be unusual on a beautifully clear late summer day in early September, I dismissed that thought and went back to bed. I got up about 15 to 20 minutes later and turned on the television and learned that an airplane had struck the North Tower of the World Trade Center. At that point, no one knew that it had been a terrorist attack. I was relatively unconcerned about my own safety because I remembered that a B-26 Army Air Corps bomber had hit the Empire State Building just after

World War II without much damage being caused to anyone, but the people on the affected floors. When I looked out the window, I saw that fire trucks and emergency vehicles had assembled on West and Liberty Streets. There was no panic evident, and they seemed to be going about their business in a calm and professional manner. I called my wife, Stephanie, to reassure her that I was alright, since I expected her to be watching the "Today Show" on NBC. But, I did not reach her and left a voicemail message that I was "fine."

A few moments later, there was a huge explosion above me, and fireballs rained down into the street. Almost immediately the television was showing pictures of a plane flying into the South Tower of the World Trade Center. At this point, I realized that there had been a terrorist attack upon our country. The World Trade Center towers had become a symbol of America's worldwide financial power and prominence, and, in a larger sense, a symbol of America. Terrorists had even tried to attack it unsuccessfully once before in 1993 by driving a truck packed with explosives into the garage below the Marriott Hotel and setting it off. The hotel was so badly damaged in that attack that consideration was given to tearing it down. But, an engineer came up with a solution to forge a single continuous I-beam through the center of the building at the third floor to reinforce the structure.

Despite the realization that terrorists had struck New York's two largest buildings, I did not feel insecure or threatened. After all, I thought to myself, this was going on 80 floors above me and terrorists would have no interest in attacking a Marriott by flying a plane into it. Rather, my immediate thoughts were on my noon meeting. I was still in my underwear and needed to shower, shave and get dressed. Having done that, I stood before the television watching the news reports that now confirmed that this was no accident but a terrorist attack. Being a former federal prosecutor, I next thought that I need to pack all my trial materials back into their boxes and litigation bags, since it was unlikely that the police or FBI would allow me back into the hotel, but would declare the site a crime scene. And that is just what I did. I began to pack my belongings. That may seem silly in retrospect, but there was never a fire alarm or public address announcement warning guests to leave the building, at least that I heard. I have since read that fire alarms are not activated in terrorist incidents because the alarms may be wired to a bomb detonation device.

Just as I had finished packing up all the trial materials in the boxes and litigation bags, I thought to myself, "How am I going to get these out of here?" As I was reaching for the phone to see if I could get a bellman to help me, the building began to shake violently as if an earthquake had hit New York City. At that moment, I looked up and out the window of my room and a curtain of steel and concrete rained down from the sky and turned the day pitch black. I have a mental image engraved in my mind of that window, with the top half black, with falling debris, and the bottom radiant with sunlight. It is like a mental snapshot of a curtain coming down. And, indeed, it was a curtain falling on America's sense of security from the rest of the world's turmoil. I did not know it at the time, but this was the South Tower collapsing onto my hotel.

I immediately turned away from the window and ran to the center of my room in order to get away from the falling debris. The room continued to shake, the building swayed, and debris continued to fall. It was like being in a building taking artillery fire. I then moved from the center of the room to the opposite wall, which I pressed myself against. I thought I had met my end, and prayed that if I were going to die that something hit me on the head and end my life in an instant. It was not the thought of dying that terrified me, but the thought that the floor would collapse beneath me and I would fall 19 floors to the ground and die in agony.

I remember thinking how remarkably calm I was in the face of what I believed to be imminent death. Then I thought that I would not live to see my daughter, Catherine, who was engaged two weeks before, get married; or see my grandchildren born. I also thought that, in retrospect, calling my wife, Stephanie, and leaving the message that I was "fine" would turn out to be a cruel joke; and that stopping to shower, shave, and pack was a mistake that would cost me my life.

Then my life passed before me, as I thought, "Have I lived a good life? A life that my parents would be proud of?"

When the building stopped shaking and the debris finished raining from the sky, incredibly I was still alive. While the room was in a shambles, the floor and the ceiling had not collapsed. I rushed out of the room forgetting my briefcase, my luggage, the boxes and litigation bags, which I had so diligently packed, and which were so important to me just a few moments before. When I got to the hallway, it was pitch black as the electric power to what remained of the building had failed and smoke and ash filled the hallway. I recall seeing light at the end of the hallway. I now know that that light was daylight, as only a few feet further down the hallway the center portion of the building had collapsed under the weight of the South Tower falling down upon it.

I called out: "Is there anyone here?" And, I heard a reply, "Come this way." A fireman lying in some rubble in the fire stairwell was shining a flashlight. I followed that light and I was able to find my way to the fire stairs. He instructed me to get out of the building, as soon as possible. I remember commenting to him, "You don't have to tell me twice," and bolting down the fire stairs. On the way down, I passed at least three firemen going up. I remember thinking how valiant and unselfish they were to place themselves in harm's way for people they did not know and would probably never know.

When I got down to the fire staircase between the fourth-floor and third-floor landings, I found that the stairwell was blocked with rubble and debris. I could hear people talking on the third floor landing, just a few feet below me. I yelled out to them: "Is anyone there?" and they replied that they were guests at the hotel and were trapped on the third-floor landing as the stairs from that point downward had completely collapsed. I began to remove debris and was able to remove enough of it so that I could proceed down to the landing. On that landing, I met two other men who were guests at the hotel. From the landing, I could see that the stairs had collapsed from that point to the ground floor. There was a huge hole in the wall at the third-floor landing on the Liberty Street side of the building, an east-west cross street that traversed Manhattan from the East River on the east side of the island to the Hudson River on the west. You could see directly out onto Liberty Street and across to St. Nicholas Greek Orthodox Church. I learned months later that St. Nicholas Church collapsed in the wake of the South Tower's collapse, but as I remember it 15 years later, I remember St. Nicholas Church still standing. I assume I was either in shock, or have mentally filled in a blank in my memory.

Liberty Street was covered with debris, and two cars were burning in the parking lot next to St. Nicholas. The pedestrian bridge covering West Street, which runs north and south on the west side of Manhattan Island, allowing access to the World Financial Center across from the World Trade Center, had partially collapsed and the emergency vehicles and fire trucks, which I had seen minutes before lined up on Liberty and West Streets, were now covered in rubble. One of the ambulances had collapsed under the weight of the debris.

Below us, about 10 feet down, on a ledge on the second floor, was another man, who I later learned was the hotel's banquet manager. Debris was still falling from the sky, and myself and another man grabbed ahold of the banquet manager's extended arms and pulled him up to the landing between the second and third floors. We all introduced ourselves to each other. One man seemed older than me, but I was not really sure since everyone was covered with white dust and powder, and everyone's hair looked gray. It was hard to assess anyone's age. I learned months later that he was a Wall Street lawyer who had retired to Florida and had come to New York to visit his old partners and was staying at the hotel. Another was also a guest at the hotel. He had a laptop computer with him. I learned years later that he was from Colorado.

I remember that when the banquet manager introduced himself to me and told me what his job was, I said to him, "I guess it will be a long time before you have any more banquets at this hotel." The banquet manager told me he had stayed behind in the hotel going floor to floor knocking on doors and telling people to get out. What a courageous man! I was sure that others had fled in terror, or others, like me, were so concerned with their own affairs that they were oblivious to what was taking place. But this fellow stayed at his post to assist in whatever way he could. That is courage!

After these introductions, the fireman who had flashed a light at me on the nineteenth-floor, joined us on the landing. I now know that his name is Jeff Johnson. A second fireman also joined us. Jeff immediately assessed the situation. He went to the hole in the wall and looked out and saw that an I-beam, which, presumably, had fallen out of the sky in the South Tower's collapse, had lodged itself on a ledge on the second floor and was leaning up against the third floor landing where we were.

Jeff got himself onto that beam and slid down it to the second floor's ledge. He then walked along the ledge toward West Street and vanished. A few moments later, he returned and announced that there was a hole in the wall on the second floor as well and that it could be accessed from the ledge. This, he said, would allow us to re-enter the building. He said that he wanted us to slide down the beam, as he had, and that we should walk along the ledge and re-enter the building on the second floor. Once on the second floor, we would look for a way out. I remember him saying: "Everyone out on the street is dead. There will be no fireman or police coming for us, if we are to get out, we have to do this on our own!"

Although I had stayed at this Marriott many times, I never noticed this ledge that I was about to descend. It was an architectural feature that wrapped around the building on the second floor. On the Liberty Street side, it was quite narrow, two or three feet wide. But as it wrapped around the building on the West Street side, it widened significantly until it formed a small patio where the hotel abutted the North Tower.

The first to climb down to the ledge was the banquet manager. He did so by sliding down the beam. I went after him, and the man with the computer came down after that. After we got down the beam and onto the ledge, we walked a few feet along the ledge and found the hole Jeff had described on the second floor. The hole was so large you could easily walk through it directly onto the second floor. There were still a guest and a fireman remaining on the landing at that point, who were about to come down the beam, when suddenly we heard a roaring freight train coming towards us out of the sky. I learned later that the sound was the North Tower of the World Trade Center collapsing with one floor caving in or another, causing a clack-clack sound as each floor fell on top of the one below it.

Jeff, who was with us, told us to hit the ground. We did. I put my hands over my head and thought to myself there is no way I can survive this and uttered a small prayer. Again, day turned to night as the debris rained down upon us. After the collapse was over, we fought our way out of the debris that had fallen on top of us and stood up. Standing next to me on my right was Jeff, to my left was the man with the computer, and to his left was the banquet manager. As I stood up, I put my hand on the arm of the fellow with the computer and he grabbed my arm. I guess we were both seeking some human comfort and kindness at that moment. The banquet manager moved over to us and put his arms around us. We stood there for a few moments locked in this embrace. Then we began to cough violently as the soot, dust, and concrete began to fill our noses, mouths, ears, and lungs. It was almost like drowning. You tried to take in air, but only managed to take in dirt and asbestos.

Once the coughing and choking stopped, Jeff took charge, and began to look for a way out of the building. The banquet manager said he thought we were in the Harvest Room, which was directly above the Tall Ships Restaurant on the ground floor. He said that there was a doorway on the other side of the room, but when Jeff climbed over the rubble to that doorway, it was completely blocked with debris. The hole that we had come through on the second floor was now completely blocked with rubble. At the time, we did not know what happened to the two other men who had been with us on the landing and were about to come down the beam. I learned months later that they too survived.

At this point, more debris began to fall and Jeff yelled that we should stand under the horizontal support beams of the building for protection. While we were seeking shelter under these beams, Jeff began looking for other ways out. I remember him pointing to a vertical structural beam in the middle of the room and saying, "We got to get the f___ out of here now. That beam is buckling. If we can't find a way out, we'll die."

Finally, Jeff found a small hole in the wall on the West Street side of the room and fished a rug from the debris, which he lodged in chunks of concrete and threw it over the side of what remained of the building and announced, "This is the way out." The fellow with the computer suggested an alternate way out, which entailed climbing down the rubble which had accumulated against the building, but Jeff said that this was the best choice. The climb down was only about 15 feet as there was at least five to ten feet of rubble at the base of the building. The banquet manager went down the rug first, I climbed down second, then the fellow with the computer, and then Jeff. When we got out onto what used to be West Street, it looked as if a nuclear bomb had exploded in New York City. The streets were devoid of human life and filled with rubble. The framing of the

World Trade Center with its grill work was embedded in the street in a vertical position. I did not stop to capture that moment, which has now been immortalized in pictures of the 9/11 attack.

Although I had been calm up to this point, I was now scared, as I did not realize that both towers had collapsed to their foundations. I thought only the tops of the towers had collapsed. As I stood there on what had been West Street, I said to myself "I have made it out, but how will I survive if the rest of the towers now collapse?" I thought, "I am in the open now, and if one of those steel beams hits me, I am dead."

As these thoughts entered my mind, I began to quicken my pace and fight my way through the rubble that blanketed West Street. There was not a soul on the street. When I got over to the opposite side of West Street, where the World Financial Center was located, the four of us, who had gotten out, reassembled as a group and proceeded over to the Hudson River, not passing a single human being. Just as we reached Battery Park City, between West Street and the Hudson River, Jeff came across another fireman he knew and they went off together. When the banquet manager, the guy with the computer, and I got to the riverfront, we found a group of policemen. One of them said that I was bleeding from the head and instructed me to get on a police boat that was moored at the Battery Park Marina, which would take me to a hospital in New Jersey, as there was no way to get to any hospitals in New York, due to the debris in the streets.

He sent the other two guys I got out with to a rest station where the Fire Department was giving out water. On the police boat, I was given a towel to wrap around my hand, which was bleeding and to mop up the blood which was coming out of my head. A few people who worked in the World Financial Center, across West Street from the World Trade Center, and who had evacuated that building, also boarded the boat. Two other firemen, one who had been overcome with the dust from the rubble, and another who had hurt his back, were carried aboard, as well. We then proceeded across the Hudson River to Ellis Island.

As we crossed the river, I looked back at the World Trade Center and noticed that the twin towers, a symbol of New York City for over 30 years, were gone. I asked one of the policemen "Where are the towers?" He said "They are gone." I said "What do you mean they are gone? I was there when the tops of the buildings fell, but where is the rest of the building?" Up to that point, I believed only the tops of the towers had collapsed; I didn't realize the entire buildings had fallen. He said, "Buddy, they are gone. They collapsed down to their foundations." At that moment, I looked to my side and I saw the Statue of Liberty, representing the past and future hope of this country. It symbolism was not lost on me.

I had gone to high school in Queens in the early 1960s and could remember looking out my classroom window and watching the World Trade Center being built. I had been in the Grand Plaza of the World Trade Center when "King Kong" was filmed. Now the realization hit me that these buildings, which I thought would outlive me by several generations, were gone.

When we got to Ellis Island, I was examined by a triage unit and told that I would be evacuated as soon as other casualties arrived. My grandparents had entered this country through Ellis Island. This was my first visit. I wondered if they could ever have imagined their grandson visiting here for the first time under these circumstances. They had come here to escape the grinding poverty and wars of the Old World, and now for the first time war had caught up with this country and their grandson.

After being examined, I found a kind young woman who allowed me to use her cell phone and called my wife. When we were connected, I simply said, "I'm alive!" then I lost the signal, so that was all I could say to her.

Unfortunately, the casualties the triage unit expected never arrived. The sad fact is that unlike me, most at "Ground Zero" didn't make it out. About 40 minutes later, I was evacuated from Ellis Island by ambulance to Bayonne Hospital, where I was stitched up and given a CAT scan which revealed a subdural hematoma. As a result, they took me to the intensive care unit where I remained for two days under observation, until they were satisfied that the internal bleeding in my head had resolved itself.

The care I received at Bayonne Hospital was outstanding. The nurses were attentive and caring. Claire, my day nurse, was especially kind to me and would come by and check on me just to be sure I was alright. Her son was a lawyer for AIG and worked in the World Financial Center. Fortunately, he got out uninjured.

One of the things that struck me while I was in the hospital was how many lives were affected by this incident. There seemed to be no one who didn't know somebody who worked at or near the World Trade Center. The female security guard who took my wallet and money clip to lock up in the hospital safe told me that her son worked at Cantor Fitzgerald, a broker/dealer, located in the World Trade Center. As it turns out, he wasn't there that day, because he was in the hospital scheduled for open-heart surgery. Over 700 people at Cantor Fitzgerald died on September 11, 2001. Her son survived the open-heart surgery and the attack on his workplace.

While in the hospital, my cousin, Leonard, and my nephew, Pat, came to visit me and stayed with me all day long lifting my spirits immeasurably. Frankly, I was having trouble coming to grips with the fact that I survived, and so many thousands had died. Both my cousin and nephew worked at the World Financial Center. Leonard, who lived on a boat in the Liberty Island Marina in New Jersey, was taking the ferry to work at the Cotton Exchange when the first plane hit the North Tower at about 8:45 a.m. The ferry turned around and took him back to New Jersey. My nephew, Pat, who lived in Manhattan, slept late, because the Monday Night Football Game, on September 10, 2001, featuring the New York Giants, had gone late the night before. When he got off the subway, the first plane had already struck the North Tower, and the police were not letting anyone walk over toward West Street. He walked uptown and eventually met my brother, Pat, and niece, Christy, at the New York Athletic Club on Central Park South.

On Wednesday, September 12, 2001, I had an MRI exam. Later that day, the neurologist told me he had good news and bad news for me. He said the good news was that the internal bleeding from the subdural hematoma seemed to be resolving itself, but the bad news was that I might have an aneurysm. At that point I called my wife, Stephanie, and told her to drive up to New Jersey, since all passenger airplanes had been grounded. It was at this moment that the companionship of my cousin and my nephew meant the most to me. I will never forget them for their kindness.

Later that afternoon, they ran another MRI and found that it was not an aneurysm. A little while later, Stephanie and my daughter, Catherine, arrived. Stephanie and I hugged each other and began to cry from the sheer joy of being reunited and seeing each other again.

Franco, a friend, had driven Stephanie up to Bayonne, New Jersey, together Catherine. The next day on September 13, 2001, I was released from the hospital, and drove out to see my parents. Stephanie, Catherine, and I had lunch with them at my sister Theresa's house, and then we drove back to Washington. While my mother was overcome with emotion on seeing me, I don't know whether my father fully understood what had happened. His Alzheimer's disease and the cancer had by that point completely debilitated him. He would be dead within two months. It was both sad and heartbreaking to see what these diseases have done to a once proud, intelligent, strong, and independent man. Then mother died unexpectedly just six weeks after my father. I survived September 11, 2001, and within three months the two people who gave me life were dead.

My brother-in-law, Tony, worked at the World Financial Center, across West Street from the World Trade Center. He told me that after the first plane struck the North Tower, all the employees in his building were told to stay at their desks. It was only after the second plane hit the South Tower that his building was evacuated. He said he was walking along the Hudson River going south toward Battery Park when the first building, the South Tower, collapsed. He then ran down the walkway adjoining the river as the dust and debris came toward him. He outran it to Battery Park.

Our drive back to Washington took us three hours from Randolph, New Jersey, to the district line at New York Avenue (Route 50), off the Baltimore-Washington Parkway. But, it took us another three hours to get from the district line to Catherine's apartment at 21st and N Streets, NW, because the Secret Service had closed many streets around the Capitol and the White House due to the terrorist attack on the Pentagon.

That same day, my son, Joseph, called me from Tokyo, Japan. He had just finished his judicial clerkship in Guam and had been in Bangkok, Thailand, on vacation before heading home, when the attack on the World Trade Center took place. Since all flights to the United States were halted after the attack, he had flown to Tokyo and was waiting for a flight home. His call was a source of great consolation. My son, Francis, who lived in St. Louis, Missouri at the time, and was on temporary assignment in Pennsylvania, drove home that weekend to be with me. Just having him around buoyed my spirits immensely. In some ways, the far-flung circumstance of my own family reminded me of the great American novels, "Winds of War" and "War and Remembrance." Although the Henry family members in the books were separated by distance and war, they remained devoted and faithful to each other.

As I write this, the thought occurs to me that the World Trade Center attack is an event that will always bind me and my family to this nation. Approximately 100 years ago, my father's parents, Pasquale and Theresa, came to these shores from Sant'Agata de Goti, Provincia de Caserta, Italy, and my mother's parents, Angelo and Rose Borgia, arrived 80 years ago from Padula, Provincia de Salerno, Italy. They were all seeking a new beginning in a new world; seeking citizenship in a new order. They were always proud of their heritage, but equally proud of the life that they had created here. I remember my grandfather, Angelo, whose name was changed to Charles by the INS at Ellis Island, being so proud to say he was an American citizen. My grandparents and my parents, Pat and Agnes Razzano, survived the depression and World War II. My father served this country in the Army Air Corps in Europe. Through the years and the travails of time, our family has built a bond with this land. And, this experience further reinforces that bond. A few years back, I was told I could apply for Italian citizenship, based on my grandparents' origins. I thought about it, but concluded not to do it. I am an American and my family is and always will be, Americans. Our country now faces a new threat of terrorism, but I rest assured each night that in time we will overcome it.

Conclusion

There is one final thought I have that I wish to convey while writing the events of September 11, 2001. It concerns the firemen who rushed into the towers and the Marriott World Trade Center, oblivious to their own safety, and intent only on saving lives. They are the exemplification of what America is. America is not about the accumulation of power, prestige, or wealth. When the terrorists attacked the World Trade Center, they thought they were attacking a symbol of America's preoccupation with material possessions. But what they found was that America means something entirely different. It means helping others. America has always been a giving, self-sacrificing country. During World War II, Americans saved the world from the greatest evil it had ever faced. After the war, we rebuilt the world, and, ultimately, by winning the cold war, we made the world a bastion where all men and women could achieve their fullest potentials. Those firemen through their self-sacrifice exemplified that American tradition.

God bless New York, a city of miracles. God bless America!

Postscript

There is a picture taken by a New York newspaper photographer of the Marriott after the South Tower fell. It shows that the entire middle of the building collapsed. On the right side of the building along Liberty Street, only a small spire of the building remains up to the nineteenth floor; the floor I was on when the South Tower fell. On the left hand side of the building, a more substantial section of the building is still standing. The photographer's camera, which captured this picture, was found in the rubble. The photographer was killed when the North Tower collapsed.

By comparison, a photograph of the hotel after the North Tower collapsed shows that the entire building was now gone, except for a small shoe box of a building on the corner of Liberty and West Streets; a few hundred feet in length and three stories high. That was the section of the building that I climbed out of. That section of the building only survived because of the huge steel beam inserted into the building after the 1993 attack in order to reinforce the building.

When I got home to Washington, I was overcome with guilt. I asked myself again and again, "Why had I survived and so many others died? " Then about five days later, I got a call from my associate, Ben, who told me that the judge in the case I was in New York on that fateful September 11th was on the phone and insisted on speaking with me. I asked if he had told her that I had just gotten out of the hospital. He replied that he had, but she had all the other lawyers in the case on the line and was insistent. I said alright, and he put her on. She took roll and then announced that we would begin trial on Monday, as the court had reopened for business. Everyone but me replied, "Ready." I asked if she knew that I had just gotten out of the hospital. She said she had, and asked how I was. I said "Fine," but explained that all my trial materials were in my room at the Marriott and were now gone. I said that there was no way I could begin on Monday. She then said October 23rd (meaning we would start trial then) and hung up. When I got off the phone, I said to my wife, "I don't care what the doctor says, I am going back to work tomorrow." While the judge may, at first blush, have sounded insensitive, in fact, it was the kindest thing the judge could have done. Rather than wallow in my depression, I went back to work and began to reorder my life by focusing on my client's problem.

In the months following 9/11, I tried to find the fireman who had gotten me out, without success. Then about a year later, my nephew, Pat, called and said that he had seen an article in the *New York Post* about a fireman who had won the Liberty Medal for saving the lives of three middle-aged men, and it sounded like my story. I ran out and got the paper at a newsstand in Washington, D.C., and sure enough the stories matched. I returned to my office and immediately wrote Jeff a letter at his firehouse. Three days later his wife, Roe, called my wife at home and said Jeff had gotten the letter, but could not call from the firehouse. However, I could call him.

I immediately picked up the phone and called him. When he got on the phone, he began to apologize about the story in the *Post*, claiming it undeservingly pictured him as a "hero." I stopped him and said, "You are my hero. If not for you, I would still be in that building figuring out how to get out." A few weeks later, my wife and I were putting the guest list together for my daughter Catherine's wedding. As we did, I turned to my wife, Stephanie, and said, "We have to invite Jeff and his wife. If not for him, I would not be here." We did and they came to the wedding and celebrated with us. I can never repay him for what he did that day for me. It is a debt of gratitude.

In the years that have passed, I have tried to reorder my life. I made the pilgrimage to Santiago de Compostela in Spain to thank God for my survival and to pray for those who did not survive. I have attended many 9/11 events and am always struck by the stories of those who did not make it out. I recall the story of a mother who spoke to her daughter on the evening of September 10th, and has had no word from her since. Her body was never recovered. The story of a wife whose husband died in the lobby of the Marriott when the North Tower fell on top of it. And, so, so many more.

I have dedicated a statute in the garden of my local parish, St. Stephen the Martyr of Our Lady of Grace in honor of all the "First Responders on 9/11." If you are ever in 19 Washington, D.C., it is right on the corner of 25th Street and Pennsylvania Avenue. I am told that many people stop and say a prayer before the statute, or leave a flower, or change.

So, how has it changed my life? I honestly try to be more understanding and patient with people. What is the use of hate or aggravation? We have to try to be more caring and compassionate to each other. We have such limited time here. But, the biggest change is that when I awake each morning, I thank God that I have lived to see my five grandchildren be born and grow! What a gift! A gift that those who lost their lives were denied. May they rest in peace.

I am one very lucky, lucky man, who believes in miracles. Thank you to that priest whom I helped to say Mass so many years ago for my personal miracle.

BRUCE SALVOG

A Minnesotan man's harrowing escape

Bruce Salvog was from Minnesota and was staying on the 20th floor of the hotel inside the World Trade Center. On the morning of 9/11, he was trapped temporarily inside the elevator of the North Tower when the first plane hit. He was on his way to the Windows on the World at the top of North tower to present a speech.

Bruce was fortunate to escape but was caught in the black smoke and dust. Although his experience was terrifying, he was amazed at the kindness and selflessness of the people he encountered. He now cherishes the fragility of life and feels grateful to be on this earth. After 9/11, he reassessed his circumstances and made the decision to retire early, so that he can spend his days helping others.

"WHAT RESONATES EVEN TODAY ARE THE INNUMERABLE ACTS OF COURAGE AND KINDNESS I WITNESSED, FROM THE FIREFIGHTERS RUNNING TOWARD THE TOWERS WE WERE ESCAPING TO THE STRANGERS ASSISTING THE INJURED AND INFIRM..."

M Y NAME IS Bruce Salvog, and I was a guest at the Marriott World Trade Center the night of September 10, 2001. I was visiting New York as part of my work in institutional investment management, and was scheduled for a "media day" to explain and promote my investment philosophy, process and track record with financial writers.

I was on my way to a breakfast speech at Windows on the World at the top of the North Tower, alone in an elevator descending from my room on the 20th floor, when the first plane hit at 8:45 am. The impact shook the elevator, which finally opened after the automatic stabilizers took effect at lobby level. We were not allowed to leave the lobby, given the chaos, falling debris and traffic mayhem outside. Some other guests said they were told to return to their rooms, but being claustrophobic, I escaped at the first opportunity to exit the rear door near the bar. I made it about a block and a half away when the second plane soared right over my head into the South Tower.

I will never forget that blue and white United plane and the massive fireball it created just behind me.

Several of us ran from there to Battery Park, where I tried to reach my wife back in Minnesota. When I finally got through to tell her I had escaped the towers but that we were apparently at war, she had no idea yet what had happened. She turned on the TV just in time to see the South Tower fall, and our conversation ended immediately since the communication dishes were atop the towers. It would be six hours before she would learn my fate.

After watching dozens jump to their deaths and the towers fall, I was trapped with thousands along the Hudson River railing in Battery Park. We were surrounded by acrid black smoke for nearly three hours.

What resonates even today are the innumerable acts of courage and kindness I witnessed, from the firefighters running toward the towers we were escaping, to the strangers assisting the injured and infirm, to the Jewish security guys who came down from the Diamond District to pass out water and masks to those with respiratory difficulty, to all those who spontaneously formed a human chain to lower people over the railing to the pitching deck of a ferry boat that would take us across the river to safety.

The spirit of selflessness was amazing.

Once the ferry dropped us in Jersey City, a fellow approached me out of the crowd to ask how I was doing, since my suit, garment bag and briefcase were still covered in a layer of dust.

Unbelievably, he was a financial writer who had scheduled to hear my breakfast speech at 9:00 am but had missed his train because his son was sick. It obviously may have saved his life. Thanks to his local knowledge and ingenuity, we managed to catch the last train out of Newark that afternoon to reach his hometown of Red Bank, NJ. I got the last available room at the Marriott there, of all places.

I wouldn't return to Minnesota until midnight on Friday the 14th, thanks to my San Diego sister who happened to be dropping off her son at Princeton. She drove me all the way to the Philadelphia airport.

Having scheduled it just prior to 9/11, I had cancer surgery at Mayo Clinic on October 10 and remain cancer free today. Still, I heard both messages.

I would later learn that mine is only one of thousands of stories of astonishing "serendipity," which are far too many to be mere coincidences. Rather, the epiphany I experienced was that there are no coincidences but that God has a plan for me that is being revealed in His time and on His terms, not mine. The fear and anger I felt are antithetical to spiritual health and can only be overcome by acceptance and faith.

What I didn't know on 9/11 but realize now is that I was spared for a reason. I retired six months later at 54. It involves - among other things - service to others: caring for aging parents, supporting widowed friends, helping at charities, sharing the joys of life with my wife of 32 years or simply doing the next right thing. It is a path of spiritual growth, illuminated by survival of 9/11.

Bruce Salvog and his wife Kathi

SIRIUS

The only police dog killed on 9/11

Sirius was a police dog killed during duty on September 11. He was a Yellow Labrador Retriever who worked for the Port Authority Police Department and was the partner of Lieutenant David Lim. Together, they patrolled the World Trade Center, including checking for explosives. Sirius spent his days protecting the people who worked and travelled through the World Trade Center complex, including the hotel.

ON SEPTEMBER, 11, 2001, Lt. David Lim left the South Tower to help evacuate people. When the buildings fell, Lt. Lim was rushed into an ambulance and brought to St. Vincent's Hospital for treatment of injuries. Miraculously, Lt. Lim was one of 16 people to survive the collapse of the North Tower. Sadly, his partner Sirius died. His remains were recovered in the winter of 2002.

PAPD Officer David Lim and his partner K-9 Sirius keeping the hotel safe for guests and employees inside the Marriott World Trade Center Hotel.

Sirius' remains were ceremoniously removed from Ground Zero with a full honor guard, in a manner befitting a hard-working member of the Port Authority Police Department.

In memory of Sirius, the police dog, his leash and Police Badge #17 are displayed in the 9/11 National Memorial Museum.

Sirius badge and training leash are displayed in the museum.

RICHARD STARK

An 80-year Florida man trapped in the
collapse meets his two guardian "Angels"

Richard Stark was 80 years old when he was caught in the rubble on September 11, 2001. He was in Room 530 on the 5th floor the Marriott World Trade Center hotel. When the towers fell, Richard was trapped in the debris and dust. He could not breathe. When he saw the demolished stairwell, he thought 'This is where I'm going to die." However, Richard was saved by Firefighter Rivera. Firefighter Rivera saved his life by leading Richard out. They slid down a steel beam from the hotel into the rubble of the South Tower to the outside. Rivera's younger partner, also named Firefighter Rivera, died while assisting in the rescue. There are various letters written between Richard Stark and Firefighter Rivera that revealed the events that took place and the bond that was forged as a result of 9/11.

"HOW CAN I EVER THANK ENOUGH FIREFIGHTER RIVERA AND THE OTHER FIREMEN, WHO PUT THEMSELVES IN HARM›S WAY TO BRING ME AND THE

OTHER STAIRWELL SURVIVORS TO SAFETY AND WENT BACK TO SEEK OTHERS?"

"WHEN WE RAN DOWN FROM THE 19TH FLOOR AFTER THE FIRST COLLAPSE, OUR BIGGEST SURPRISE WAS TO FIND YOU AND ANOTHER CIVILIAN AT THE 4TH FLOOR. WE THOUGHT WE HAD EVACUATED ALL THE PEOPLE FROM THE HOTEL."

– Firefighter Rivera

A New York City police officer leads 80-year old Florida resident Richard Stark from the rubble of the World Trade Center on September 11, 2001.

My Guardian "Angel"

After I escaped, I always wondered about the firefighter who saved my life. In mid-October, an article in *Men's Journal* mentioned the New York City Firemen in the Marriott World Trade Center Hotel on September 11th. The article mentioned Ladder Company 12 headquartered at 150 West 19th Street.

I immediately called Ladder Company 12. The Fireman who answered the phone knew immediately who the Fireman was who led an old fellow down a beam and through the rubble.

It was Fireman Angel Rivera. I spoke to Firefighter Rivera later to thank him for saving my life. Firefighter Rivera remembers very well what happened and had told everyone at the Ladder Company about the event that transpired.

He and three other firemen (Henry Kothe, Matthew Tamsey and Jason McGimpsey) went up to the top floor of the Marriott Hotel to work their way down and evacuate everyone. No one had any idea that the South Tower would collapse. When they arrived to the fourth floor stairwell, everything collapsed. When the dust cleared, they could see that several people, including myself, were trapped on the third floor landing. They skidded down through the ruins to the third floor landing and discovered that the only exit was down a beam leaning against the building. Firefighter Rivera declared that it was his responsibility to get me out.

He said the others were much younger and did not need assistance. Firefighter Rivera remembered particularly how well-dressed I was, in a blue blazer. Firefighter Rivera says he took me down the beam and about half way to the emergency vehicle. When I could walk no further, he turned me over to two policemen who took me to the emergency vehicle. Firefighter Rivera says I am his good luck charm as he considers that his life was saved because he was out of the Marriott helping me when further collapse of the Marriott would have engulfed him. He thanked me for saving his life!

He reported that five members of his Ladder Company were lost. He said the three of them died in the Marriott Hotel.

I set forth below many exchanges of e-mails with Firefighter Rivera.

October 22, 2002 - E-Mail to Firefighter Rivera

"I can' t believe my good fortune to be taken out of that situation of certain death by a NY Firefighter by the name of Firefighter Rivera and then being able to make contact with you and learn that you survived that horrible day. Your suggestion that you were probably spared by the coincidence of being occupied with helping me when it would have been fatal for you to have remained in the Marriott, also gives me pause to ponder how our lives converged at a crucial moment."

October 23, 2002 - E-Mail from Firefighter Rivera

"It was a wonderful surprise to hear from you. Ever since that day I thought of you often. I wondered who you were, where you are, how are you doing. I talked about you a lot around the firehouse and prayed that you were OK. I thought I would never hear from you. I thought I would never find out who you were. Being able to help you helped me also.

We, Firefighters, as you know for a fact our job is to save lives at any cost. Saving lives is our priority. You were there. And you became my priority and responsibility. Unbelievably by me helping you I kept myself from walking into my own death. As I told my fellow firefighters you were my God. In that tragedy even though I lost some very dear friends I am very happy that you are doing well. I would very much like to meet you and would also like you and your family to come visit at the firehouse whenever you are in town. I would like to keep in touch with you."

During November, I spoke briefly to Firefighter Rivera, but he was not feeling at all well. I understand that he is suffering some serious Post Traumatic Stress Symptoms. He was suffering tremendously from PTSD that he was not able to talk at any length on the phone. The *Men's Journal* article mentions that "Angel's having a tough time". He is suffering serious Post Traumatic Stress problems.

One of the Firemen of Ladder Co 12 explained to me that their stress won't let up. They lost five "brothers", three in the Marriott. They are kept in a constant state of grief with an unrelenting series of funerals and memorial services and new bodies being discovered. Needless to say, I expect to visit Ladder Company 12 when I am next in New York! I hope Firefighter Rivera will be recovered sufficiently to welcome such a meeting.

Meanwhile, I had been trying to contact Firefighter Rivera to see how he was doing. I feared that he was on medical leave as happened to so many other Firemen. I finally received the following e-mail:

December 12, 2012 - Firefighter Rivera's E-Mail to Me

Mr. Stark,

Thank You for your letter. I just returned to NY from vacation. I spent five days in Fort Lauderdale and seven days in Puerto Rico. I am sorry you are feeling this way. I am also not fully recovered. I guess it will take a long, long time. But we have to be brave and try.

For me the loss of my close friends, especially one whose name was also Firefighter Rivera, is hard to comprehend. I made him my responsibility and took him under my wings. Now I miss him more than anything in the world. I am trying to figure out where I went wrong. And how come, if I always made sure he was by my side at every critical situation, I let him get away from me.

Now he is dead and at times I wish I were too. He was known as little Firefighter Rivera. I am big Firefighter Rivera. Altogether we lost 5 firefighters: 3 from Ladder 12, a Battalion Chief and his aide. They were all extraordinary people. Among those, I personally lost, there were others from near by companies who were also good friends.

As I write to you my friend, my tears keep rolling down my face. Why was I left alive?

When we ran down from the 19th *floor after the first collapse, our biggest surprise was to find you and another civilian at the 4th floor. We thought we had evacuated all the people from the hotel.*

We lost our guys when they decided to go back to 19th floor to retrieve a life saving rope which at that moment seemed the only way to escape. If we had used the rope we would have all died. When they reached their destination, on the way down, one member of the other companies that were trap on the upper floors by the first collapse, regained consciousness and called out a mayday. "Mayday, Mayday"

He gave his name and company number and followed by his message

"I am trap and I am losing consciousness."

The only place he knew he was the top floor of the Marriott. On the way down my guys turned around and tried to locate him. One of the guys that was with us [and you] on the 4th floor decided to go and give them a hand. That's when your presence turned my decision. I told him that I couldn't possible leave you alone. So he said I will go, you find the way out, and let us know how. He walked one flight up, that is when hell broke loose.

First, there was the big explosion. Then, there was the sound of the rumble. The building shook like an earthquake. We thought of it as a bomb going off or even another plane hitting the building. We had no knowledge of the Twin Towers collapsing. It turned black and shook with an enormous force. I still can feel the wind rush slowly increasing.

You and I were sitting on the floor when it all calmed down. It was dark. I reached out and felt someone near me. I still couldn't see anything in the dark. When the smoke and dust cloud started to dissipate, slowly we began to see light. I wondered if that was what they call the Light and the end of the tunnel. As I told you before, your presence and I taken responsibility for you helped both of us. I also must say that I was impressed by your composure in such a critical moment. You made it easy for me to help you. You held up very well. God Bless you and your wife Barbara and your children and grandchildren.

I must say something else. Days after September 11th, my colleagues, trying to give me courage said to me to think about the gentleman I helped and to think how grateful that man and his family will be to you. It all comes back.

Thank you for effort in trying to contact me.

I am grateful. I wish you strength and good health and also to your family too. And if there is one thing that is pure joy in this whole tragedy is that I was able help you.

So it is up to you now to keep well and have good life.

Your friend forever,

Firefighter Rivera.

At Christmas time, I sent Firefighter Rivera a gift. He responded immediately with his thanks, but said that if I would not object too much he would like to turn that gift over to the 12th Ladder Company's fund for widows and children of fallen Firemen

My eternal gratitude to Firefighter Rivera

How can I ever thank enough Firefighter Rivera and the other Firemen, who put themselves in harm's way to bring me and the other stairwell survivors to safety and went back to seek others? In conversations and exchanged e-mails with Firefighter Rivera since that terrible day, I have come to appreciate that Firefighter Rivera is not just a Fireman "doing his duty". His concern for his fellow Firemen and the beneficiaries of his efforts far exceed expectations. His generosity and humility are endearing and admirable qualities.

How can I thank Guil and Karen enough for putting aside everything for two days to rescue and resuscitate me? And my Darien family, Sally and Rick, who provided loving care for me for several days? And how can my soul ever forget the thousands of innocent people who perished in that holocaust of violence?

The expressions of love and concern from my family and friends have been overwhelming and humbling. I even received kind words of concern from my recent litigation adversary. Through it all, I am having difficulty explaining or accepting that I am alive while so many perished. I understand that some survivors even experience feelings of guilt. I don't suppose I will ever reconcile my understanding of God's love with the existence of so much evil and hatred in this world.

I am told that many people who suffer similar experiences are never really free of their horrible memories. And I am learning the hard way that "post-traumatic stress disorder" is not a trivial condition and can be painful and distressing, lasting perhaps for months, or even a lifetime in case of Firemen and some Vietnam veterans. Barbara, who is herself a psychological counselor, insisted that I obtain therapy, which has been helpful. Among other things I have learned that my symptoms are "normal" and will over time disappear.

In some ways, I have the uncomfortable feeling that I have been attending my own funeral. But I thank God for myself and my family that I survived. This experience underscored for me the importance of my beautiful life with Barbara. We have been dramatically reminded that our days together are numbered and that opportunities for hugs and kisses should not be missed.

Sadly, as in the case of Pearl Harbor, which my generation remembers so vividly, our world will never be the same. From now on, time will be measured as either «Before WTC» or «After WTC».

Firemen's Fund

John, one of my close friends, was one of the investors in our venture involved in the litigation settled on September 10. He decided that my nearly fatal experience was the result of a trip to New York on behalf of the venture partners. So he solicited contributions from our venture participants in my name for the NY Firemen's Fund. I am most appreciative of John's action and the generous contributions of many of my partners.

The Return Home

After restless nights and several days of unsuccessful efforts to get on a plane for Florida, Sally and Jim took me to LaGuardia Airport on Sunday morning, September 16, 2001. They put a sandwich in my pocket and remained with me for the two or more hours it took to negotiate the long, long line of apprehensive travelers. When they left we agreed that I should call them on my cell phone if my flight was ultimately cancelled, as so many had been over the past few days. I traveled really light as I had no baggage! The Delta flight was only 25% full as many people were reluctant to fly. CBS interviewed me at the curb and asked if I was worried about flying. I said that after my experience at the WTC, flying was the least of my fears.

My final homecoming to Barbara was a tearful event to say the least. I doubt I'll ever leave her again, although I am thankful she was not with me on this occasion.

BILL VAUGHAN

*A husband and wife from Virginia struggle
to make sense of life after 9/11*

---

*Bill Vaughan was the Chief Economist and Demographer from
Virginia traveling on business to NYC to attend the NABE
conference. He was on the 15th floor in his room inside the
Marriott World Trade Center Hotel when the attacks occurred.
He was in Room 1526*

"WE STRUGGLED TO MAKE SENSE OF THE MANY
STRANGE SIGHTS AND SOUNDS —BODIES DROPPING
AMID THE COILS OF TOILET PAPER STREAMING OUT
IN RIBBONS DOWN THE SIDE OF THE BUILDING,
THE TINKLING OF SHATTERING GLASS, THE
BRIGHT, BEAUTIFUL AUTUMN MORNING. THE
TOTAL UNREALITY OF THE SITUATION MADE US
FEEL LIKE A PAIR OF EXTRAS IN SOME GROTESQUE
HORROR MOVIE."

WE WERE STAYING in Room 1526, which looked out over West Street about halfway between the main elevator and the stairs leading down to the cocktail lounge. I was preparing to go down to the final meeting of the conference I was attending.

My wife, Laurel had just left the room to work out at the fitness center on the top floor of the hotel. She was waiting for the elevator when the first plane struck.

I was drinking coffee and looking out over West Street. After the explosions, as the building swayed, questions ran through my head—was it an earthquake, an industrial accident? But because of the earlier incident years before, I decided it must have been a bomb. Fearing that the elevator might have been destroyed, I threw the door open only to find Laurel running toward me.

The fire alarm was blaring. All around, we could smell smoke and hear debris hitting the building. I told Laurel, "I think it was a bomb." She replied, "No, an airplane crashed into the building—I heard the engine. I looked out the window overlooking the plaza and saw flaming debris raining down into the plaza."

Laurel wanted to retrieve her purse, which she had locked in the safe. She tried in vain to recall the combination. Finally, I grabbed my wallet and told her, "We have to leave—we'll get our stuff later." Off we dashed, never dreaming what was awaited us.

We ran down the side stairs closest to West Street, encountering only one other couple struggling with their bags. We believe we were some of the last guests to leave the hotel. As we had done all weekend, we headed toward the plaza exit. Fortunately, we were stopped by a hotel employee who directed us to exit through the side doors facing Liberty Street. Out on the street, a police officer directed us to "run as fast as you can and don't look up."

I remember the clear blue sky was filled with floating paper like a weird ticker-tape parade. All around us people were displaying emotions ranging from horror and shock, to disbelief and bravado—crying, laughing, and shrieking. All range of human reactions to a scene too immediate and nightmarish to really understand. We, the fortunate ones, bore witness to unbelievable and seemingly unreal events occurring several hundred feet above us. We could do nothing but helplessly stand and watch or turn away.

I remember feeling small pieces of debris peppering my hair and something wet landed on the side of my face.

We struggled to make sense of the many strange sights and sounds — bodies dropping amid the coils of toilet paper streaming out in ribbons down the side of the building, the tinkling of shattering glass, the bright, beautiful autumn morning. The total unreality of the situation made us feel like a pair of extras in some grotesque horror movie.

Standing at the corner of West and Liberty streets, we could hear the engine of the second plane roaring nearer and nearer. As the building exploded, we, like the rest of the crowd, ran for cover.

I can still hear today that wave of a collective moan working its way from Wall Street down Church and Liberty streets, emanating from the throats of the thousands pouring out of adjacent buildings.

Time became meaningless—escape was our primary concern.

People and their activities whirled around us in a blur of impressions. Some trying to keep up the appearance of calm as they ducked under an awning to nonchalantly talk into cell phones. Being stopped by a Japanese news crew already set up for interviews. Joggers and bicyclists flitting by, determined to finish their morning workout while unwittingly heading directly towards the burning towers. The sidewalks littered with hundreds of discarded shoes. Cars parked on sidewalks with groups huddled around the blaring radios, "...another one is on the way—six are unaccounted for..."

A relentless stream of vehicles conveying the first responders, their faces momentarily in focus before speeding by. The sound of alarms of every type, all clanging at once and uninterrupted. And, of course, that cruel blue sky, so sharp and clear beyond the black smoke and red flames.

As we came up to the Hudson River, I was considering jumping in. My wife—seemingly on instinct—turned uptown towards the apartment of my elderly aunt and uncle, the only people we knew in Manhattan, who happened to live uptown near the George Washington Bridge.

For some time, as we ran, then trotted, then walked up West Street, Laurel kept asking, "We'll get back into our room, don't you think? Maybe tomorrow, when this is all finished?" I don't know how I knew, but I did know that the towers were coming down.

As we walked, a new wave of human chorus followed us and overtook us, wordlessly signaling that the South tower appeared to be tilting. Now five or six blocks away, we turned and watched as it gracefully melted down to the horizon. Lucky for us, we were upwind of the debris cloud.

After walking to midtown, most of the frenetic activity had ceased, save for the emergency vehicles still periodically rushing by. We decided to try to flag a cab. The first one we saw stopped and the driver was wonderfully sympathetic, helping us find my relative's address. In typical Yankee fashion, he still charged us cab fare.

When we finally located my Aunt and Uncle's apartment, around 11:00 AM, we were able, after a few tries, to get an open circuit on a pay phone nearby. They knew we were staying at the World Trade Center hotel since they had met us downtown for lunch the day before. Breathlessly, I announced to my uncle on the other end of the line, "Frank, we're alive, we made it out alive!" After a long pause, Uncle Frank replied, "That's nice…"

We learned later that my aunt and uncle had spent the entire morning of September 11, 2001 in blissful ignorance of the chaos occurring only about four miles away.

Laurel and I spent a sleepless night watching the stream of emergency vehicles crossing the George Washington Bridge and holding onto one another.

We were fortunate enough to catch a train out the next morning to arrive at Union Station in D.C. the next afternoon, as the black cloud still hung over the Pentagon.

In the years since that fateful day, we have struggled to make sense out of the senseless – seeing a grief counselor, volunteering in the community and joining the 911 Hotel Survivors group. One fact about that day makes us marvel and that fact is that somehow, some way, at every turn, coincidence and dumb luck (or some would call it our guardian angels), combined to keep us safe and keep us together.

JANIS WILLIAMS
A California woman with PTSD

Janis Williams is from California and traveled to New York for business. She was staying on the 11th floor of the hotel. She describes the day as frightening, and suffered from frequent nightmares after 9/11. Janis still has post-traumatic stress and feels her life had changed forever after that day.

"THE SIGHTS, SOUNDS AND SMELLS OF NEW YORK WERE STUCK IN MY HEAD BUT LIFE WAS GOING ON AROUND ME. THE NIGHTMARES CAME EVERY NIGHT…I COULD NOT CONTROL MY EMOTIONS."

ON SEPTEMBER 11, 2001, I was staying at the Marriott World Trade Center on a business trip for the State of California Treasurer's Office. I was there with another Treasurer's Office manager. Since 9/11, I have never been able to remember my room number but I think it was on the 11th floor. I was close to the North Tower overlooking the West Side Highway.

On the morning of September 11, I was getting ready for the day when I heard a loud explosion. The hotel moved as if we were having an earthquake but it was different. I went to the window and looked out. I could see a lot of paper and debris falling from above. When I heard all the sirens, I carefully went back to the window and saw the emergency vehicles.

I was very scared and thought there was something seriously wrong. I put on some pants, shoes and a jacket over my nightgown. Even though I was scared, I thought I would be back in my room after a few hours so I grabbed only my room key. I didn't want to waste time, so I left my purse and valuables in the safe.

As I was going down the stairs, I tried to go out an exit to the plaza but realized that wasn't safe. As I reached the first floor, I saw firefighters and police in the hotel lobby setting up what I can only describe as a command center. The police and firefighters were being instructed to go into the hotel and south tower. They instructed me to leave from an exit away from the North Tower.

When I got to the exit, a police officer was there. A few people were in front of me. He told each of us to wait until he could see if it was safe, then run across the highway as fast as we could to a grassy area. He also instructed us not to look up or stop for anything. When it was my turn, I ran.

When I got to the other side of the highway, I was standing with a small group of people under a building overhang. I looked up and saw the hole in the North Tower and the smoke. No one said what had caused it.

Then I saw people jumping or falling from the tower. The only words spoken from the people around me were "Oh my God, oh my God, oh my God." I joined them in shock and prayer.

I just couldn't watch. I knew it wasn't safe to stay there. I hadn't been in New York in over 30 years. I got turned around and ended up on the West Side Highway again near Liberty Street by the South Tower. I heard an airplane, looked up and saw it go over my head. I couldn't comprehend what was happening until it hit the tower. The explosion was frightening.

As I moved away, a man in military fatigues said "That's it, we are at war. It's no accident that the first tower was hit by a plane and now another plane hit the second tower. It's an act of terrorism." That was the first time I understood what was happening and I was frightened. I knew I had to find a safer place. I knew I would die if I stayed there. Surprisingly, there weren't many people on the streets so I again wasn't sure where to go.

I don't know exactly how far away from the South Tower I was when I heard a roar, saw it collapsing then saw the debris cloud racing down the street towards me. I hit the ground. It's true your life passes before you when you think you are going to die. All I could think about was my family. I could hardly breathe and my glasses and clothes had a dust all over them. I looked up and realized I was alive. It was eerily quiet.

I finally made my way to Battery Park but I didn't know where to go from there. When I heard a loud noise and people screaming, I turned and watched as the North Tower collapsed. I was standing with a group of people who worked at the Stock Market. They offered to help me find a way off the island. We were told all the bridges were closed and the only way out was the Staten Island ferry. When the ferry stopped, a line of men and women with search dogs got off. We knew they were going to look for the dead, injured and those who had survived. I couldn't help but cry.

We got on the ferry. It was mostly empty. When we arrived at the Staten Island ferry building, we were not allowed to go inside. I think they were afraid we were contaminated. We were able to take a bus for a few miles, but there were cars parked at the bus stops blocking the roads. I realized the people standing around were waiting for their loved ones to return. After a few miles of walking, we arrived at an apartment. I was able to call home, talk to my family and let my office know I was safe. I was relieved to find out my coworker had made it safely out of the hotel too. I spent the night with the group. The next day my office made arrangements to have me picked up by a coworker that lived in Connecticut. I stayed with his family.

When I left New York, I had nothing but the clothes I wore out of the hotel and my room key. We rented a car in Connecticut since there was no other way to get home. We left for California on Thursday night, September 13. We drove nonstop until we got to Cheyenne, Wyoming. We rented hotel rooms but couldn't sleep so we left after about 5 hours. I just wanted to see my family. We arrived home in Sacramento, California on Saturday night, September 15.

It felt surreal being in California. The sights, sounds and smells of New

York were stuck in my head but life was going on around me. The nightmares came every night. I also had memory lapses, and crying spells. I could not control my emotions. I was diagnosed with post-traumatic stress disorder. I was not the same person. I knew my family was going through an adjustment period with me. My husband was my rock. My young children realized the mother that left for New York was not the mother that returned. I struggled to move on, so I pretended to be "normal". People wanted to hear my story but didn't realize how hard it was to talk about it.

The State of California Victims of Violent Crimes Division established meetings for California families who lost loved ones on the planes and in New York and for the California survivors of the World Trade Center. I heard stories from the families and saw pictures of their loved ones killed in the terrorist attacks while at the meetings. They had arranged for counsellors for us. I felt guilty for surviving when so many had not.

The survivor group was small. It was good to talk to others who had similar experiences. The meetings helped me understand I needed to talk about what I had seen, felt and experienced on 9/11 so I could heal and cope with my life that had changed forever.

What happened on 9/11 still affects me. If I hear a plane, I have to know where it is. I still have trouble sleeping. I'm sensitive to the sound of sirens. I've made many new friends since 9/11, but I've told only a few that I was at the WTC.

I have learned many things from being at the WTC on 9/11. Foremost, I am grateful for the love, support and patience of my family. I truly value my time with family and friends. I plan things I've always wanted to do and I do them. I know I have been through an indescribable experience and survived. I know PTSD exists and I will always have it. I've learned to fake it until I can make it through any situation. I know I will go back to New York someday because I think it will help in this journey of being a survivor. Every year I think maybe next year but then change my mind as the anniversary approaches.

Janis Williams
Sacramento, California

TOM WITT

*A West Virginian University Professor is
separated from his wife for hours*

---

*Tom S. Witt was from West Virginia and traveling to NYC to
attend the National Association for Business Economics' annual
meeting at the World Trade Center Marriott Hotel. At the time,
Dr. Witt was the director of the West Virginia University Bureau
of Business and Economics Research, where he also served as a
professor of economics. His wife, Grethe Myles, accompanied
him on the trip and was in their room on the 10th floor (Room
1040,) when the first plane crashed into the North Tower.
They were finally reunited after 4 p.m. Tuesday, having spent
six hours separated, not knowing the status of each other. A few
months after the attacks, a police officer found Tom's belonging
in the wreckage.*

"I RECEIVED A PACKAGE IN DECEMBER FROM THE
NYPD WITH PERSONAL EFFECTS RECOVERED AT
GROUND ZERO, HARDLY THE END TO A STORY THAT
LINGERS IN MY MIND TODAY."

O N 9/11, I was at the World Trade Center Marriott Hotel (situated between the two towers) attending the annual meeting of the National Association for Business Economics and listening to the president of Morgan Stanley, when the chandeliers in the ballroom began to shake.

Sensing danger, the nearly 400 attendees headed for the exit and eventually made it out the east side of the building. I found a pay phone and called my office, only to look up and see the second plane fly into the South Tower. Hanging up the phone in shock and not knowing where my wife was, I started looking for help.

We gathered a group of economists (two women and four men) and proceeded to slowly walk up to Morgan Stanley's Times Square offices where I was able to contact my office at noon, but they had no information about my wife's whereabouts. From Morgan Stanley, we traveled to the Bank One mid-town offices where we got some food and made calls.

Shortly thereafter I learned that my wife was OK, having escaped down 10 flights of the Marriott fire escape. Once she reached the plaza level, she was directed to the underground shopping plaza where she felt the second plane crash. She exited the east side, walked past the Brooklyn Bridge and Chinatown, and met two other strangers and walked across the Manhattan Bridge to a car wash in Brooklyn. The proprietor allowed her to call my office.

When I finally found out that my wife was alive and our relatives knew as well, I spoke with the press, beginning with Beth at West Virginia Public Broadcasting. Playing back that interview takes me back to the emotions we all felt during this time of national tragedy. I met an executive with the Bank of Montreal who took me into his home in the West Greenwich Village, where I was reunited with my wife around 4:00 p.m.

Needless to say, it was a very emotional reunion.

We left NYC on Thursday on a train to Pittsburgh. As we exited a tunnel in New Jersey we saw the smoke from the WWTC site, followed by our last view of the city—the Statute of Liberty.

I received a package in December from the NYPD with personal effects recovered at Ground Zero, hardly the end to a story that lingers in my mind today.

About the Author

Joyce Ng is a survivor of the 9/11 attacks. On September 11, she was traveling to New York City on a business trip and was a guest at the Marriott World Trade Center hotel. As a young adult, she witnessed a major event that forever changed her life. On 9/11, when the first plane crashed into the North Tower of the World Trade Center, she was in her room in the Marriott. The plane's landing gear fell onto the roof of the building, and the hotel caught on fire. While the hotel was burning, debris was falling around the area, and she witnessed people getting killed or injured.

Since then, Joyce founded a non-profit charity to unite survivors from this building. In the forefront of the 9/11 community, she serves as the voice of 9/11 survivors nationwide, bringing awareness to the physical and emotional trauma endured by those who survived the attacks.

All proceeds from the sale of this book go to the non-profit 501(c)(3) charity
"September 11 Survivors of Three World Trade Center"

Made in the USA
Coppell, TX
29 March 2023